FLEXIBLE LEARNING:

Evidence Examined

Mike Hughes

Network Educational Press Ltd

Network Educational Press Ltd
PO Box 635
Stafford
ST17 OJR

First Published 1993
© Copyright Network Educational Press Ltd
ISBN 1 85539 013 2

Bound in Great Britain by Redwood Press Ltd, Pegasus Way, Bowerhill, Melksham, Wiltshire.

Contents

ACKNOWLEDGEMENT

Flexible Learning: Evidence Examined is a summary and evaluation of developments in teaching and learning styles in Geography teaching at Balcarras School, Cheltenham, that have taken place during the last five years.

It has been compiled by pupils, teachers and parents, and reflects upon life in a real school and work done with ordinary young people.

I would like to thank many people who have shown me support and encouragement during the development of flexible learning: the staff, senior management and governors at Balcarras; the pupils, past pupils and parents whose thoughts form a major part of the book; the Geography Department at Cheltenham Sixth Form Centre for their contribution, and colleagues in the South West Flexible Learning Project.

I hope that the book will stimulate interest in, and generate discussion about, effective classroom practice, so that ultimately it may benefit those who matter the most - the pupils.

Mike Hughes
February 1993

INTRODUCTION

Flexible Learning: Evidence Examined is the sixth book in the Teaching and Learning Series from Network Educational Press. The book details the work of the Head of Geography at Balcarras School, an 11-16 Comprehensive School in Cheltenham, where a serious attempt has been made to evaluate the classroom approaches that are described in the earlier books in the series.

In Books 1-5 a clear set of principles and working practices for effective teaching and learning were established.

Book 1   *Flexible Learning: An Outline* presented a clear rationale for flexible approaches in the classroom, particularly in relation to the National Curriculum, post-16 developments, and assessment and recording procedures.

Book 2   *Classroom Management* showed how flexible approaches require high levels of classroom organisation, the development of pupils' independent and group skills, and the effective use of resources and space.

Book 3   *Resources for Flexible Learning* showed how existing resources can be modified to provide more clearly for differentiation, variety of approach, more structured assessment and for the integration of cross-curricular skills and themes. The use of study guides is explored.

Book 4   *Tutoring* looks at the benefits of using small group tutorials, describes ways in which such groups can be managed and organised, and looks closely at tutoring styles and techniques.

Book 5   *What Makes a Good School* argues that successful teaching and learning requires good leadership, a supportive environment and the kind of management strategies that bring out the best in pupil and teacher alike.

What is unique about the developments in Geography at Balcarras School is that it is the only example, of which we are aware, of a teacher who has implemented all key components of flexible learning, and then systematically recorded outcomes.

Mike Hughes, in his teaching of Geography, has adopted both the philosophy and practice of flexible learning:

- the rationale of the teaching is based on the small group tutorial and around individual action plans
- resources are well organised and study guides are used to help pupils manage their learning
- clear strategies for classroom management are in place
- the whole initiative has been supported by senior management and governors.

What makes this case study exciting is that other teachers in the department have continued to teach in a more traditional way with groups of similar ability so that the flexible learning initiative could be evaluated.

Mike Hughes has therefore been able systematically to record the results of flexible learning in his classroom over a four-year period and to compare it with results in other classes.

He has collected details on:

- the perceptions of pupils
- 'pencil and paper' test results
- examination results
- take-up for post-16 Geography
- views of former pupils now studying for a degree in Geography
- attitudes of parents.

The results show what can happen to pupil attitude, work practices and achievement once flexible learning is fully implemented.

The findings are, of course, unlikely to satisfy the rigorous demands of the academic research community. Nevertheless, they cannot be ignored and we hope that further research will be stimulated by this book.

One final point needs to be made. There are politicians and sections of the media who constantly denigrate approaches such as those described in this case study. They will use phrases such as 'trendy' and 'progressive', and assume that because the teacher does not stand in front of the class lecturing the whole time the pupils are therefore not being sufficiently challenged and learning is unstructured and *'laissez-faire'*.

The approaches used by Mike Hughes and described in this book are not 'woolly'; the so-called 60s approach of abandoning pupils to discover for themselves does not happen. What is happening is high quality teaching and learning which is producing high standards of achievement and motivation. Those politicians and 'advisers' from right-wing think tanks who are having an increasing influence on education, should reflect on this. They should take note not only of the evidence in this book but also from those best placed to understand how learning actually happens - HMI. Eric Bolton, Chief HMI until 1991 and an inspector for 19 years is in no doubt:

> The evidence from inspection is that poor standards of learning are more commonly associated with over-direction by teachers, rather than with teachers opting out and allowing pupils to set the style and pace of learning. Time and again in HMI reports, whether concerning bright or not so bright children, older or younger pupils, academic or practical lessons, the criticism is that teachers over-direct, over-determine and unduly narrow the scope and focus of what is being studied, or undertaken, with the consequences that the achievements of the pupils are limited and depressed.

Eric Bolton, from 'Education: Putting the Record Straight' (16 articles from leading figures defending education against attacks from politicians and the media), Network Educational Press, 1992.

Chris Dickinson
Rob Powell

Editors

1

Reasons for Change

REASONS FOR CHANGE

During the last few years, a time of rapid and significant change in education, there has been a substantial review of the teaching and learning experiences that go on within the Geography department at Balcarras School.

This review and subsequent debate have been the result of a number of factors and include:

- Dissatisfaction with the limitations of traditional methods and a subsequent rejection of continuous whole-class teaching

- GCSE

- TVEI

- National Curriculum

- Flexible Learning Project.

Dissatisfaction with the limitations of traditional methods and a subsequent rejection of continuous whole-class teaching

Although external influences undoubtedly gave the development of teaching and learning styles some impetus, the initial stimulus for reviewing the classroom experiences of pupils studying Geography at Balcarras came from within. It was based on the principle that it was not *what* we taught but rather *how* we delivered the subject that was of paramount significance.

This desire to review and revamp the Geography provision at the school was largely a result of a dissatisfaction with, and a rejection of, more traditional approaches to teaching. These were seen as being relatively ineffective; a view that was based upon experiences both as a classroom teacher and tutor. Pupils appeared generally bored and uninterested and seemed to spend long hours passively receiving information.

As children receive in excess of 10,000 hours of formal education it seems very sad and something of a waste that the majority of pupils seem to be bored and switched off by much of the work they are asked to do. Why is it that enthusiastic and eager 11-year-olds become disenchanted and uninterested teenagers by the time they are14? How much of this is inevitable and how much is due to the diet provided in the majority of 'traditional classrooms' nationwide?

It was apparent that many children were arriving at secondary school used to groupwork and working independently only to encounter classroom situations which actively discouraged the same degree of collaboration and participation. Thus the skills necessary for independent study and for accepting increased responsibility were not being developed and in many cases actually eroded during the first few years of secondary education.

It was against this background therefore that the learning approaches currently employed with young people studying Geography at Balcarras began to evolve and the day-to-day classroom experiences were developed.

GCSE

The introduction of the GCSE examination in 1988 brought two fundamental changes to the teaching of Geography at secondary level. Firstly *the nature of the examination* required candidates to analyse a large amount of information from a variety of sources. This meant that the memorisation of facts and the associated learning by rote was an inadequate preparation for the new exam and that pupils needed to be encouraged to think independently. Secondly, the *coursework* component of GCSE required pupils to carry out individual investigations appropriate to their ability. Many Geography teachers recognised the need to modify the way Geography was delivered in the early years of secondary education in order adequately to prepare children for the different demands of study at GCSE level and to equip them with the necessary skills for independent investigation.

TVEI

One of the most significant effects of TVEI, or as it is known in Gloucestershire, the 14-18 Curriculum Project, has been to focus thinking on teaching and learning styles across the curriculum. In particular, it has encouraged pupils to play a rather more active role in their learning and has subtly modified the role of the teacher from one of formal instructor to tutor. The TVEI mission statement talks about equipping young people *'for the demands of working life in a rapidly changing highly technological society'* and goes on to say that one way in which TVEI does this is by *'enabling young people to learn to be effective, enterprising, and capable at work through active and practical learning methods'.*

This fundamental objective of TVEI is reflected in the aims of Balcarras School, one of which is to *'assist pupils to acquire knowledge and skills relevant to adult life and employment in a fast-changing world'.*

It is difficult to see how these goals, which few would argue with, can be adequately achieved with a total diet of formal, whole-class teaching, and consequently they provide further encouragement for teachers to review existing practice.

The National Curriculum

The overhaul of the teaching styles employed by Geography teachers in Balcarras began before the birth of the National Curriculum. Flexible learning methods were originally employed as they were considered effective and therefore desirable. However, the precise nature of the National Curriculum would appear to make flexible learning a necessary response to the requirements of the statutory orders.

Differentiation

As our work has been exclusively concerned with the delivery of Geography to secondary school pupils it is appropriate to analyse the nature of the statutory requirements for the subject in the National Curriculum. Consequently the following statements have been extracted from the final orders for Geography, although it is important to point out that the same or similar statements appear in all of the proposals to date.

> Schools should bear in mind that the objective of the National Curriculum is to ensure that each pupil should obtain maximum benefit, by offering pupils the opportunity to reach the highest possible achievements but without making impossible demands.

(Geography in the National Curriculum 1991)

Clearly, the flexible learning framework provides pupils with an opportunity to work at their own pace, address their individual needs, and to stretch themselves to their personal limit, making the achievement of maximum potential far more likely than it would be in a more traditional classroom with pupils engaged in a common task.

Differentiation is at the heart of the National Curriculum, and it is clear that individual children will be working at different levels in a number of attainment targets in a cross-section of subjects.

Although superficial analysis may conclude that the National Curriculum requires that pupils should be placed in sets according to ability, a more detailed appraisal of the legislation would recognise that individual pupils will be at different levels and will have different needs even where sets have been established.

It is extremely difficult to see how a whole-class approach would ensure that

> individual pupils are acquiring knowledge and understanding which enable them to work at appropriate levels.

(Geography in the National Curriculum 1991)

or how pupils working outside the range of a particular key stage might be accommodated within a class of children of the same age, as this would necessitate the particular child being

> given work on an individual basis.

(Geography in the National Curriculum 1991)

However, one of the key principles underpinning the flexible learning methodology employed at Balcarras is that teaching and learning should take place at an individual level rather than be directed at a group of pupils, ensuring that the requirements of the National Curriculum, with its emphasis on differentiation and individual progress, can be fully met.

Assessment

A second key feature of the National Curriculum is the particular emphasis placed on the role of assessment. Although the profession still awaits decisions and guidance about the precise nature and style of National Curriculum assessment, statements in all of the statutory requirements and the latest information from SEAC suggest that the flexible learning framework enables assessment to take place in a manner and for a purpose intended by the current legislation.

When the following statements are considered

teacher assessment should be an intergral part of teaching and learning.
(Teacher Assessment at Key Stage 3, SEAC 1991)

assess pupils' achievements and subsequently focus their teaching plans on the particular needs of individual pupils.
(Teacher Assessment at Key Stage 3, SEAC 1991)

Involving pupils in assessing their own work helps them understand better their own strengths and needs.
(Geography Non-Statutory Guidance, NCC 1991)

it is clear that the assessment procedures that are a significant component of flexible learning delivery are necessary features of assessment in the National Curriculum. If teacher assessment is to be an integral part of teaching and learning it is necessary for the traditional role of the teacher to change and evolve. They must be freed from a reliance on whole-class teaching and the daily administrative chores associated with the classroom to enable them to work intensively with individuals and small groups of children as part of normal lessons.

The formative and diagnostic nature of assessment that is a feature of flexible learning approaches facilitates individual target-setting by pupils. Such strategies will be required if assessment in the National Curriculum is to lead, as intended, to teachers planning lessons based on the particular needs of individual pupils.

TGAT reinforces the point, arguing that the assessment process should provide both *'feedback and feedforward' (National Curriculum Task Group on Assessment and Testing: A Report)*, and it is the planning of future action based upon the identification of individual strengths and weaknesses that highlights the crucial role that diagnostic assessment can play as a means to an end rather than as an end in itself.

Interestingly, the notion of children being involved in self-assessment is encouraged by the National Curriculum as a way in which pupils' understanding of their own strengths and weaknesses can be made more effective in precisely the same manner as the self-assessment procedures promoted by flexible learning.

As this particular style of learning has developed at Balcarras, the emphasis has been on quality and depth of understanding rather than breadth. Consequently, the large amount of content included in the statutory requirements for Geography will require a slight change in emphasis, and from that standpoint it could be argued that the imposition of a content-overloaded National Curriculum will reduce the effectiveness of young people's learning in the subject.

However, to a certain extent this will be true in whichever manner the National Curriculum is delivered, and to reject flexible learning in favour of a more teacher-directed approach simply to ensure brisk coverage of the orders not only disregards how much of the material individual pupils have absorbed and understood but also fails to take into account some of the inherent advantages of the flexible learning structure.

Most notably, flexible learning allows a greater quantity of work to be covered during a given period both as a result of greater pupil motivation and a corresponding increase in effort and because valuable time is not lost waiting for other pupils to finish a particular exercise. The fact that the methodology allows pupils to work at their own best pace means that more able pupils will be able to forge ahead, and it is my experience that vast quantities of work are produced while low attainers are able to consolidate their understanding at a lower level.

It should be remembered that it is not expected that all children will complete all of the National Curriculum. Why, therefore, should children who have not yet reached level four be subjected to level five and six material simply to 'cover the syllabus'? Clearly, this is not the intention of the National Curriculum and yet it is the inevitable outcome of any attempt to drive all children through all the prescribed content.

Flexible learning ensures that not only will pupils be working at a pace and level suitable for their needs, but also that children who are capable of reaching the higher levels will be able to do so. Indeed it is hard to see how the National Curriculum can be delivered effectively and in the manner in which it is intended by any other teaching strategy.

Flexible Learning Project

The Flexible Learning Project was the final piece in the Balcarras teaching and learning styles jigsaw, pulling several strands together to provide a coherent structure for daily classroom practice.

In short it provided:

- a framework for teaching and learning

- a support structure of advisers and colleagues throughout the region who shared a similar vision

- funding, which provided invaluable time for preparation and reflection.

Prior to the project, the influences of the factors outlined had led to a rejection of much existing practice and an acknowledgement of the need to involve pupils to a far greater extent in their learning. This process had already begun, and with some success. The introduction of flexible learning methods such as individual action-planning and small group tutoring undoubtedly increased the effectiveness of young people's learning in Geography. It not only took the development of teaching styles to its logical conclusions but also made individualised learning and support far more systematic and structured.

The decision to pilot flexible learning approaches was therefore made on a firm philosophical basis. The decision to use these approaches over a period of time in the classes of one teacher only was made on two counts:

1) to enable the school clearly to evaluate the approach before using it with all geography classes, and
2) to allow colleagues less confident of flexible learning approaches to observe it in action and to decide if and when to adopt the approaches themselves.

In the chapters that follow, therefore, readers should be aware that 'flexible learning in Geography' refers to the teaching Head of Department, Mike Hughes, and not the department as a whole.

2

Flexible Learning in the Geography Department

15

FLEXIBLE LEARNING IN THE GEOGRAPHY DEPARTMENT

Flexible Learning

The term, flexible learning, is not one single approach to teaching; rather, it is a structure that encompasses a wide range of teaching and learning styles that are employed within an overall framework.

Aspects of individual learning, resource-based learning, supported self-study, research and project work, enquiry and open learning are all found under its umbrella. So, too, is formal teacher instruction, although this method of delivery is used rather more sparingly than in a more traditional setting and is often confined to lead lessons, introductions and to the conclusion of a unit of work.

The development of flexible learning in the Geography department at Balcarras will be described in detail in this chapter. In Section One five key components will be examined:

   1) Key Principles

   2) Tutoring

   3) Resources and Study Guides

   4) Classroom Management

   5) Differentiation.

Section Two will then describe how these key areas of flexible learning are applied to teaching of Geography in years 7 to 11.

Section One The Principles and Methods

1) Key Principles

Although difficult to define, flexible learning is essentially a student-centred approach and was underpinned at Balcarras by the following key principles:

   • *Pupils should take increasing responsibility for their learning.*

   This should be done in accordance with the age and ability of the pupils, their previous experiences and the task in hand.

- *Teaching and learning should take place at an individual level rather than be directed at a group of pupils.*

  This should take into account the pupils' age and abilities, their specific learning needs, their personalities and the pace to which they are best suited.

- *Pupils should be made aware of how they learn and how specific learning activities contribute (or otherwise) to their progress.*

  Pupils should be able to identify which learning strategies are effective for them.

- *Pupils should receive close support and guidance on a regular, planned basis through small group and/or individual tutorials.*

  Encouragement and advice are essential if pupils, due to the individualised nature of the work, are not to become isolated.

Not only was this approach designed to make teaching and learning in geography more effective, it was also consciously aimed at making it more enjoyable. It was felt that enjoyment was all too often neglected by schools and its importance more readily acknowledged by pupils and parents than by teachers.

The simple model that when pupils are enjoying themselves they will work harder and that increased effort will lead to greater success, and therefore greater enjoyment, was held to be valid and thought to perpetuate itself. It was also recognised that the reverse could also be true. Pupils who are struggling and/or bored can easily switch off, and a lack of effort can lead to increased learning difficulties and further rejection.

Greater involvement of pupils in their studies and an increased responsibility for their own learning was thought likely to prove to be enjoyable for the majority of children and that the corresponding improvement in motivation would set the upward spiral in motion.

By the time pupils are studying for GCSE it is anticipated that they will be able to accept a good deal of responsibility for their learning and progress, and in order for them to do this effectively it was considered vital to develop the skills and attitudes that are necessary for independent study from an early age. The notion that only pupils of a certain age, notably 'A' Level students and beyond, can study in this way was rejected. Indeed it was felt that many traditional approaches to secondary education failed adequately to prepare pupils for the demands of study at 16+.

The work of the Geography department was deliberately designed to build upon the experiences provided by many of our feeder schools and to foster and develop the pupils' role in their own develpment from Year 7 onwards.

Factors Affecting Choice of Style

Within this framework the precise nature of the teaching style employed will be adapted to meet the requirements of individual needs and specific situations. The strategy adopted will be determined by a multitude of factors, which include:

- the age of the pupils
- the ability of the pupils
- the nature and content of the work
- the length of the lesson
- the time and day of the lesson
- the previous experiences of the pupils.

Thus low-attaining Year 8 pupils will be engaged in significantly different activities last lesson on a Friday afternoon than a top GCSE set during the first lesson on a Wednesday morning, but both will work within a flexible learning framework.

Doubts are occasionally expressed regarding the effectiveness and suitability of flexible learning in certain contexts. In particular, concern over this style of working for young children, low attainers and for specific subject areas are common causes of scepticism and even rejection. However, this rather superficial analysis fails to take into account the essential flexibility of the methodology and the modification of classroom practices to cater for individual situations. Thus, rather than rejecting the approach as ineffective or unsuitable for a particular context, consideration should be given to how the learning strategies encompassed by the flexible learning structure can be modified to accommodate a set of specific requirements.

2) *Tutoring*

Tutorials are regular, planned meetings between the teacher and a small group of between 4 and 6 pupils, although occasionally tutorials are held on an individual basis. It was quickly acknowledged that tutorials are the key to effective flexible learning and, as such, great emphasis and importance was placed on them. As pupils become more experienced in tutorial situations, so the nature and organisation of these meetings alter.

Key Features

The following are the key features of the tutorial provision for pupils studying Geography at Balcarras:

- Tutorials are part of normal lessons although a pupil or a group of pupils may organise an extra tutorial out of lesson time if there is a specific need. While the tutorial is taking place, other members of the class are engaged on their individual action plans.

- Clear ground rules are established from the beginning and include:
  - i) no one from outside the tutorial group may interrupt while a meeting is in progress
  - ii) children must be polite and remember other people's feelings. Any comments or criticism must be constructive and made within an atmosphere of cooperation.

- Normally the seats are arranged in a circle. No one, including the teacher, is therefore in the dominant position.

- Tutorials are normally chaired. Initially the teacher acts as chairperson, but as the children become experienced with this way of working they take turns at chairing the meetings.

- Tutorials normally have an agreed and clear agenda. Sometimes this involves asking each group member, 'What do you hope to get out of this meeting?' or by writing down, 'By the end of this tutorial I hope to achieve ………'

- Although all tutorials are conducted within this framework they tend to fall into one of five categories, normally as a result of the stage a particular group has reached in a unit of work.

Types of Tutorial

Clarifying tutorials. If flexible learning approaches are to be successful pupils must have the confidence and ability to work independently. Without this confidence they will constantly interrupt the teacher for help and reassurance.

The clarifying tutorial is therefore crucial. Once a task has been set, this kind of tutorial is vital in ensuring that everyone has a clear understanding of the task, is confident of how it might be tackled and that clear expectations have been set. Teachers in whole-class teaching who rely on pupils owning up to being unsure are fooling themselves. Young people are more likely to share doubts in a small, secure, group tutorial.

These kinds of tutorials are often merged with planning tutorials.

Planning Tutorials occur at the beginning of a module. Pupils bring along a rough version of their action plans and discuss their proposals with the teacher and the rest of the group. It is during planning tutorials that the teacher ensures that each individual pupil is covering the key areas of the unit, is using suitable resources, is being stretched, is working towards realistic goals and is generally working at a level suitable for his/her ability.

Subject-specific Tutorials are an integral part of the teaching and learning process. There are occasions when specific geographical concepts are best explained by the teacher in the role of subject expert. Such tutorials can either be initiated by the teacher or can occur as a response to a pupil or small group of children who are experiencing difficulties with a particular aspect of the subject.

These subject-specific tutorials form an integral part of the learning process and largely replace whole-class lessons. Instead of addressing the entire group, only the pupils who actually need help or have reached the relevant stage in their work are engaged while other pupils are free to work on tasks more suitable to their particular needs.

The benefits of this approach include the following:

- Exposition is generally more effective with small groups and can be pitched at a level suitable for the group in question.

- Pupils are much more likely to ask questions and admit to difficulties in a small group.

- The teacher can, through skilful questioning, assess if all the pupils have grasped the subject matter, and she/he can, of course, respond accordingly. This immediate assessment of understanding is not possible in a whole-class situation simply because of the numbers involved.

General Progress Tutorials are held during a unit of work and are planned in advance. Extra tutorials can be called at any time by either the pupils or the teacher. During the tutorials a combination of the following activities will take place:

- Work to date will be reviewed and evaluated, and plans for further study will be developed.

- Pupils will discuss their progress with one another and with the teacher.

- The teacher will ask questions about the work produced.

- Pupils can ask the teacher or one another questions about the work.

- Ideas on presentation and information about suitable resources will be swapped.

- Pupils can raise any problems that they are experiencing and specific difficulties can be ironed out.

- The timescale of the project will be reviewed.

Pupils should therefore leave the tutorial having had opportunities to voice their ideas and opinions and also to listen to other people's points of view. They should be clear about the way in which their work should progress and should feel encouraged to continue with their studies.

The teacher should be clear about how the individuals in the group are progressing and should have detected and sorted out any misunderstandings or specific problems.

Assessment Tutorials occur at the end of a unit of work and often involve two separate meetings. Pupils will have previously completed their self-assessment forms which centre on two key statements: *'Aspects of my work that I was pleased with'* and *'Aspects of my work that I could have improved'*. (See Appendix E).

Pupils will then comment on their work and on the work of others in the group, within the framework laid down by the ground rules. The teacher will ask questions, make comments and offer alternatives and generally make the assessment process more effective and meaningful for the individual pupil. The emphasis is on pupils' understanding of why a particular piece of work was effective or unsuccessful and on their recognising and fully understanding their own particular strengths and weaknesses.

Following the initial meeting the teacher will complete the marking of the work and add comments to the assessment sheet. When possible, this is done in the presence of the individual pupil, so that any comments or observations can be fully explained. When this process is complete the teacher and pupils talk through the comments on the assessment sheet to ensure that individuals are clear about the progress they have made.

At the conclusion of assessment tutorials each individual pupil sets out his/ her targets for future action.

3) Resources and Study Guides

If teachers are to able to find time to conduct small group tutorials it is self-evident that other pupils in the class need to be working on their tasks with confidence. Many of the tasks that they will be engaged in will require them to make use of resources of varying kinds - books, media, software, equipment - and resources therefore need to be carefully organised and managed. These resources are available and accessible in either the classroom or library resource centre.

Study guides play an important role in helping pupils to organise their tasks, resources and general planning (see example in Appendix C). They provide a framework and structure, advice and stimulus and enable the pupils to work independently without constant reassurance from the teacher.

4) Classroom Management

If teachers are to find time for tutorials they must not only organise resources but also consider classroom management.

There is no one correct way to manage a classroom, even within a flexible learning situation, and the following description is only one alternative way of organising a room. It is a system that proved appropriate for the specific context, and was designed to

- free the teacher from the daily administrative chores such as giving out paper, responding to requests for equipment, etc.

- make groupwork the norm while allowing all pupils to see the front.

To these ends the following management strategies were adopted at Balcarras:

- Pupils had open access to resources.. All basic resources such as paper, crayons, glue, rulers, etc. were housed on a mobile trolley which was located in the centre of the room during lessons and locked away for security purposes after school. Procedures for returning resources and keeping the trolley tidy were established from the outset.

- Tables were arranged so that pupils could sit in groups of six with no pupils having their backs to the front of the room. It was important for pupils to become used to sitting and working in groups, and yet all could see the front for lead sessions.

- Furniture was not regarded as static. It was easy to rearrange the desks to suit the specific requirements of the lesson.

- Small work areas were established on the landing. These comprised a small number of individual desks and a coffee table and easy chairs which were suitable for group discussions. Tutorials were often held here.

- Small groups which needed to watch a video could do so in this area without disturbing the rest of the class.

- Extensive use was made of the library resource centre. Not only were the resources themselves extensively used but the extra accommodation proved invaluable.

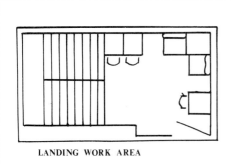

LANDING WORK AREA

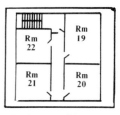

GENERAL LOCATION

A PLAN OF ROOM 19

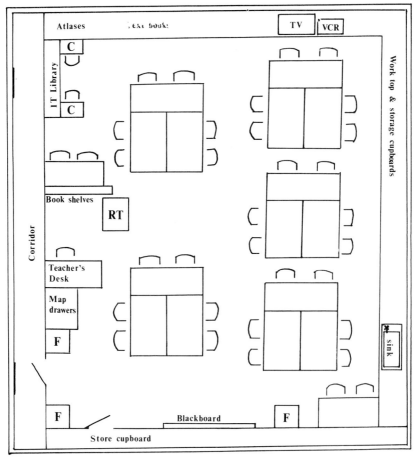

RT = Resource trolley   C = Computer   F= Filing cabinet

- For the first few minutes of a lesson the teacher was available to talk to pupils, deal with specific requests, etc. When these minor matters had been dealt with the teacher was generally able to conduct tutorial sessions or to work with small groups.

5) Differentiation

Although differentiation has long been an issue, particularly in mixed ability situations, the nature of the National Curriculum has elevated its importance to unprecedented heights. Teachers are being faced with the prospect of catering for a wide range of ability, even within a setted situation, to ensure that every pupil has the opportunity to attain the highest possible achievements. Not only is the profession being asked to address the needs of slow learners, it is also being challenged to stretch the most able pupils and from an early age. Within these two extremes there are a large number of children traditionally labelled 'average' who are entitled to be provided with opportunities to achieve their full potential.

More than ever before the belief that all pupils have special educational needs holds true, and more than ever before differentiation is an issue in urgent need of being addressed. This is a daunting prospect and, within a traditional, whole-class setting, a largely unmanageable one.

On the other hand, differentiated learning activities are the inevitable outcome of a flexible learning approach that incorporates small group tutoring and individual action planning.

There are three main ways in which differentiation can be achieved, depending on the particular circumstances.

Differentiation by resource. If teachers are able to collect a rich selection of resources for any one topic, it will be possible, through the careful use of tasks and study guides, to direct pupils to resources that are appropriate in terms of language level, ease of use and design.

Differentiation by task. If tasks are created separately from resources then the teacher can cater for a wide range of ability:

- core compulsory tasks, and extension tasks

- tasks that support pupils with learning difficulties
- tasks that challenge able pupils
- tasks that involve group cooperation and peer support.

Differentiation by task can be successfully used both for short-term tasks and, if differentiated study guides are used, for the longer-term, extended tasks.

Differentiation by support. There are a number of ways in which differentiation by support is possible. If teachers make regular use of small group work the potential for peer support is enormous. (See some of the comments made by pupils in Chapter 3.)

In the tutorial, teachers are also able to guide pupils, modify tasks, provide challenge where appropriate and generally meet the needs of individual pupils. For example, pupils may all be working to the same overall learning objectives, using the same study guide. The negotiation of individual action plans will allow pupils to interpret the study guide in the most appropriate manner. The objectives of the unit may be the same but the manner and depth to which these objectives will be achieved can be negotiated in the tutorial.

Where agreement has been reached between a pupil and teacher on a particular task, this is recorded in the pupil's action plan. This enables each individual to react to previous assessment and to set personal learning targets - a key aspect of differentiation.

Section Two

In Section One of this chapter the key components of flexible learning were outlined. In Section Two the application of these key areas in the Geography department at Balcarras is examined, with particular reference to how they operated in different year groups.

Year 7

If pupils are to be required to take an increasing amount of responsibility for their learning, it is clear that they must be introduced to the skills and attitudes necessary for independent study from an early age. The Year 7 course, therefore, is an induction into this style of learning and is designed to prepare pupils for increasing autonomy in later years. There is a deliberate attempt to build on the work of the primary schools, and pupils are encouraged to think for themselves and make individual decisions.

The key features of the Geography provision in Year 7 are:

- From day one the emphasis is on enjoyment and active participation with pupils being encouraged to learn.

- Individuals are encouraged to work at their own best pace on tasks suitable for their ability. This will include the stretching and challenging of the able pupils.

- Pupils are encouraged to make decisions, however simple, for themselves. Their opinions and feelings are valued.

- Much of the work is based in small groups with pupils being encouraged to discuss with one another tasks and possible solutions to problems.

- Pupils often help one another with specific difficulties. Not only do pupils who have failed fully to grasp a point benefit by receiving an individual explanation in 'their language' but also the pupils doing the explaining are forced to organise and articulate their thoughts, thus promoting deeper understanding.

- Key atlas skills are introduced and developed during the first half term. They include latitude and longitude, the use of the index, the contents page and a guide to the variety of maps and other sources of information available.

- Within the first few weeks pupils will be able to choose a suitable atlas and find an appropriate source of information for the task in hand. They will never have atlases or books given out to them and will never be told to turn to a specific page.

- Pupils will be introduced to note-taking techniques, which involves identifying key points and noting them down. They will be encouraged to develop their own note-taking style.

- Much of the work is organised around a series of key words. These include *describe, explain* (pupils should always be aware of the difference) *why? how? where? when?* (pupils are encouraged to ask these questions about all topics).

- The organisation of small groups allows the teacher to work intensively with a few pupils every lesson. Not only does this develop excellent personal relationships, it also enables the teacher to assess very quickly the individual pupil's understanding of the work being covered and deal with any gaps in knowledge accordingly.

- Pupils will have the opportunity to choose when they do their homework tasks during the week. Advice is given on organising personal time, drawing time lines, meeting deadlines, etc.

- As the year progresses pupils will be involved in extended pieces of work which include a degree of choice over what is covered, when it is done and how it is presented. Pupils are not allowed to take 'soft' options.

- Pupils will be introduced to the idea of self and peer-group assessment. Pupils are encouraged to comment on their effort, enjoyment and attainment.

- Teacher assessment takes place in conjunction with pupil assessment. Individual strengths and weaknesses are identified and future work planned accordingly.

Years 8 and 9

Following their experiences during Year 7, pupils will be encouraged to take much responsibility for their learning during Years 8 and 9.

By Year 8 it is anticipated that individuals will have been introduced to and will have developed the skills, attitudes and competencies necessary for independent study. It is, however, acknowledged that this is a continual process and that some children will develop at a faster rate and at an earlier age than others.

The following are the key features of the teaching and learning styles adopted with Year 8 and Year 9 pupils:

- Pupils are introduced to a unit of work (normally a 6-week block although occasionally modules last a term) and have the task of producing an individual *action plan.* (See Appendix A.)

- Action plans include references to specific areas of study, resources to be used, methods of presentation and the length of time the work will take.

- A booklet, '*A Step by Step Guide to Writing Action Plans'* was produced (in conjunction with a group of pupils) and supports children during this stage. (See Appendix B.)

- Units of work are often presented in the form of a study guide which provides pupils with a framework in which to work. (See Appendix C.)

- Study guides state clear learning objectives for the module and offer suggested resources that are available in the classroom and library/resource centre. Usually they would include a number of compulsory activities and a series of optional tasks.

- Initially pupils receive a significant amount of assistance when compiling action plans, usually through small group discussion. As the pupils become more experienced, the amount of help they need gradually reduces.

- Pupils are responsible for locating and selecting suitable resources, although key texts, videos, etc. are always highlighted on the study guide. A departmental resource catalogue (compiled by pupils) is an invaluable aid during this stage. Extensive use is also made of the library resource centre.

- When pupils have completed rough versions of their action plans they attend a tutorial.

- During the tutorial individual action plans will be discussed and finalised. Pupils will be expected to explain and justify their proposals in addition to having the opportunity to ask questions and share ideas and resources with the rest of the group.

- During the tutorial the teacher will ensure that each individual pupil is covering the key areas of the unit, using suitable resources, being stretched and generally working at a level suitable for his/her ability. This a challenging experience - aiding confidence and understanding.

- Once the action plan has been discussed and negotiated, it is finalised, signed by pupil and teacher and a deadline agreed.

- During the course of Year 8 pupils will discuss how various learning activities help their understanding. They are introduced to the working of the left and right brain and are aware of the significance of colour and visual images. Copying in any form is totally rejected - pupils are encouraged to change the form of information whenever possible, i.e.: turning a piece of writing into a labelled diagram, describing a map, turning figures into a graph, etc. The emphasis is always on identification and presentation of key points with particular attention paid to the key words introduced during Year 7.

- Pupils will then put their plan into action, planning their own activities for the week, including homework. Activities are planned and subsequently recorded in a *log book*, which is signed each week by the teacher, who has the opportunity to check that work is being done and make any appropriate comments regarding the quality of the work. This constant monitoring enables staff to detect quickly any problems or lack of effort or, alternatively, work of high quality. (See Appendix D.)

- The teacher is therefore freed from the whole-class role and is able to work with a small group of pupils in a tutorial situation. Tutorials present an opportunity for clarifying, monitoring progress, dealing with specific difficulties, offering advice for future study, sharing ideas, encouraging, assessing and coaching.

- Units of work are concluded with an *assessment tutorial*. Prior to the meeting each pupil will have completed a *self-assessment sheet* which revolves around the two key headings: *Aspects of my work that I was pleased with* and *Aspects of my work I could have improved.* (See Appendix E.)

- The teacher adds comments to the assessment sheet and explains/ discusses the relevant points with the individual concerned. During an assessment tutorial pupils assess and discuss other pupils' work in a friendly, constructive way.

- The outcome of an assessment tutorial is an agreed target for improvement/attainment in subsequent units of work and will form the starting point for the next action plan.

Years 10 and 11 - GCSE

The experiences in years 7-9 have been designed deliberately to prepare pupils for a significant degree of independent study at GCSE, with pupils at Balcarras following the SEG A syllabus.

The following are features of the teaching and learning that takes place in the delivery of GCSE Geography at Balcarras:

- Units of work are based around the nine units of the GCSE syllabus.

- Work often involves a series of lead lessons with follow-up activities differentiated to meet a wide range of abilities. These activities are presented in the form of study guides.

- Pupils are expected to accept much responsibility for their learning and for organising their studies.

- Key resources and concrete examples are suggested.

- Pupils work through the activities at a pace and level suitable for their abilities.

- The teacher is freed from continuous class teaching and can work with small groups of pupils in a tutorial situation; often this involves 'subject-specific' tutorials.

- Pupils employ individual note-taking techniques which have been developed lower down the school. The emphasis is on identification and learning of *key points* and is based around the key words and questions introduced during Year 7. (*Describe, explain, why? where? how? when? because.*)

- Many pupils employ *mind-mapping* techniques, often with individual variations. Some choose to use A4 paper to make notes, others prefer small record cards, while a number of pupils have committed the notes to audio-tape, to enable them to play back material when doing their paper rounds.

- Pupils will be aware of the working of the right and left brain, the use of colour and the importance of visual imagery. A good deal of time is devoted to learning 'how to learn' and a number of techniques are suggested.

- The emphasis is on *learning* and *understanding* material from the very beginning rather than accumulating notes for two years and then revising prior to the examination.

- Copying or dictation in any form is totally rejected by the pupils as being boring and relatively ineffective.

- The pupils are aware that making rough notes during a lesson and then connecting these to finished notes immediately after the session ensures that the same material is passing through their brain a number of times. Organising rough notes and interpreting scribble forces the pupil to think carefully about the material that has just been covered. They can quickly identify any aspect of the work that they do not fully understand and act accordingly.

- Pupils usually work in small groups and are constantly encouraged to discuss the work with one another. They are frequently required to find out information and discover solutions to problems. Often specific queries and difficulties can be dealt with by other people in the group. Not only does this help the person who has a problem, but it also forces the person who is doing the explaining to organise and clarify his/her thoughts.

- Many pupils choose to employ the 'revising techniques' that are covered when discussing ways in which people learn. This involves going over the key points of the work at intervals of five minutes after completion, the evening that the work was completed, the day after, one week after and one month after. The key points act as triggers to the person's memory and regular revisiting enables the pupil to learn and remember material effectively.

Flexible Learning at Balcarras: Conclusions

Once these five key components as described in Section One are in place flexible learning can really be effective.

One of the most noticeable and pleasing outcomes of flexible learning is the way in which the most able pupils are really stretched. They are not held back by whole-class teaching but are free to progress at a pace and to a depth that really challenges them. The standard of the work that has been produced during the last few years has been consistently high, with much of it outstanding. Indeed, a small number of Year 8 pupils were successfully introduced to geographical concepts more normally associated with 'A' Level Geography, while a small number of Year 10 pupils are able to sit GCSE a year early.

There is no doubt that the precise nature of the National Curriculum creates many problems for secondary school geographers and that the huge content overload significantly increases the difficulties of delivering key stage 3 along flexible learning lines. However, it is clear that the vast quantity of content creates enormous problems irrespective of teaching style employed. There is, though, an understandable temptation to resort to a teacher-centred, whole-class approach to learning simply to 'cover the syllabus' and a feeling that the sheer volume of material precludes a flexible learning approach. This is misguided thinking on two counts: firstly, reliance on a whole class, didactic approach does not ensure quality, differentiated learning, and secondly experience has shown that the problems of coping with the National Curriculum are actually reduced by adopting flexible learning techniques.

In particular, flexible learning

- allows pupils to progress at their own best pace so that more able pupils are not held back.

- enables pupils to start working immediately they enter the classroom rather than waiting for late-comers, the teacher, etc. (Five

minutes wasted at the start of each lesson amounts to around seven
hours lost per year.)

- ensures that homework activities are much more closely aligned
with National Curriculum schemes of work.

- increases motivation to such a significant extent that pupils spend
longer, and therefore cover more material, on homework.

- ensures that all pupils are always working at a level and pace
suitable for their ability.

The temptation to rush through the material simply to cover the syllabus is
no guarantee that all pupils are genuinely learning and understanding the
work, and pupils' attainment and subsequent SAT results will suffer as a
result. All teachers and departments must be conscious of producing high-
quality SAT results as a response to the increasing emphasis placed upon
such performance indicators, and it is clear that the best way of ensuring
success in examinations is by promoting quality, in-depth understanding
throughout the course.

Much is presently being made of the need to raise standards and to increase
pupils' expectations, although conspicuous by its absence is the guidance
about how this may be achieved. One need look no further than flexible
learning for a system of classroom management and differentiated learning
that enables the standards of all pupils to be raised. This is the case for
those of low ability and for the so-called 'average' pupil. The most dramatic
gains, however, are for pupils of high ability.

3

Perceptions of Flexible Learning

PERCEPTIONS OF FLEXIBLE LEARNING

Pupils' Perceptions

Over a period of time pupils have played a significant part in fine-tuning the procedures and learning styles adopted. Discussions, as part of regular tutorials or as impromptu chats, generated many ideas for modification and improvement. Their views were valued and actively sought in a manner which contributed to the feeling of ownership they had for their learning and further increased the responsibility they were given for their progress.

In true flexible learning style the headings that appear in this evaluation were decided upon by the pupils themselves and then completed independently. A summary, written in their own words, is presented below.

Year 8 Pupils

Why do we do it?

We work like this because it is more enjoyable and because of this we work harder and learn more. I'm not quite sure why we do it but I think that I use it to help give myself independence. The teacher can look at us as individuals rather than as a group.

How do we do it?

Before we start a unit we write an action plan to show what we want to achieve. The teacher helps us to do this. This means we have targets to reach and when we've finished we assess how many we have reached and what we could have improved. The teacher also assesses our work and lays out the things that we must cover.

We come into a lesson and immediately start work rather than wait for the teacher to tell us to start. We know exactly what work we have planned to do and how long it's going to take us.

How is it different?

It is different from traditional teaching because of the way we work to our own ability and needn't cover what we already know. Instead of teaching (as such) the teacher talks to us individually

*or in small groups about the work we are doing and how much
we are learning.*

*We choose our work, presentation and resources instead of the
teacher or textbook doing so. We work more freely and
independently.*

*We decide for ourselves what we do in the lesson and set our own
homework. As soon as we come in to the lesson we start, we
don't wait for the teacher to tell us to start. We don't copy off
the blackboard as in other lessons. We can find information out
for ourselves. We work at our own speed but have to cover
certain aspects of the topic we're doing. The teacher doesn't
stand at the front and tell you what to do.*

How is the content and presentation decided?

*We get to choose the contents of the project quite freely although
there are certain things that we have to cover. The presentation
is totally up to us. This can be anything from a booklet to a
video-tape. We get a lot of independence here.*

*Some activities are compulsory and others are optional. We can
also choose activities of our own. Work is usually done on A4
file paper but we can also use other ways to present our work,
such as posters, tapes or videos.*

What resources are used?

*The resources are important. Base resources are suggested,
such as videos, books or a computer database. After that,
resources are chosen by us. I always use an atlas somewhere.
Sometimes people are good resources.*

*We have videos, books and software that we can refer to. Other
resources are available in the library resource centre. Although
some resources are given to us, we are expected to find out a lot
of information for ourselves.*

How are we assessed?

We assess ourselves at the end of each topic and also the teacher assesses us.

We assess ourselves by using our action plans. We give our comments and so does the teacher. A tutorial is used to give an overall assessment. We say what we were pleased with and decide together what could have been improved. I like the way we assess ourselves.

Because we normally work in small groups it is easy to assess our work by comparing it with that of other people during a tutorial which the teacher is sometimes involved in. They also write comments on our work. Together we set targets for the next unit. You get good ideas from other people during tutorials.

What are the advantages of flexible learning?

It gives us responsibility and independence. We get to choose a lot. I find that I can push myself more by knowing what I'm going to be doing in the next five or six weeks.

It is much better in the way that we have more choice on what to do and we can work at our own level of ability. I like it a lot and because I enjoy it I work much harder than normal. I think everyone does.

I like working at my own speed. Because I can take my time I make fewer mistakes and my work has improved. I like setting my own homework. I can usually do something in more detail than I would in school. I always do more Geography homework than the school guideline.

It is not boring as a lot of other lessons are. Normally, I find the work easy but in Geography I don't have to cover what I already know because we are all doing different things.

We have all done loads more work than in other subjects. I

*think I have learned a lot and have already filled a file. I am
really surprised at the amount of work I have done.*

*I think the biggest advantages are that the teacher talks to us as
individuals and that if we have a problem he can help. We don't
have to waste time doing the same things as everyone else.*

How does this style of learning benefit you outside of Geography lessons?

*It makes us more independent and responsible and this helps us
in other lessons.*

*We know many different ways to present our work. It has made
me more imaginative. Because we have to work in key points I
understand things better and know what kinds of information
should be included.*

*I am much better at finding out information and doing research.
I now know where to look. Mainly it has given me more
confidence in what to do.*

*I am always thinking about how the things I am doing in lessons
are helping me learn. I have much more self-confidence when I
am in school. My dad says I have much more confidence when I
am at home. In the home it makes us more independent.*

Are there any drawbacks to this style of learning?

*Not really, but there is more work for the teacher (because we
produce more).*

*It would be possible for people to abuse the system if they
wanted but I have never known that to happen as everyone
enjoys working like this. Anyway, I can't imagine that the
teacher would let this happen.*

*It has made me wish that we could work like this in some other
subjects.*

Can you think of any ways in which the system could be improved?

Not really, although I wish that we could have double lessons. Single periods are not really long enough.

I think that parents should be included on the assessment part of the action plan.

Year 11 Pupils

How do we work in other lessons?

We have never really been told how to learn anything. We are just expected to go over the work and remember it.

We are often told to learn things for homework or revise for a test, but how? Nobody teaches us how to learn.

We are usually told things and only rarely are asked to find things out. Some lessons involve lots of copying from the blackboard or having notes dictated to us. We are then expected to learn them.

We often have to listen to the teacher. Either that or work out of books. Sometimes this involves copying notes. Some teachers give out sets of notes and tell us to learn them. I know some pupils who don't bother reading them.

I often think that we do too much during lessons. I have so much information that I can't possibly remember it. It would be a lot better if, for homework, we could just have time to go over what we did in class.

Information is just drummed into us and we are told to learn it or else get detention. Teachers give tests on what we have done and keep you in if you don't get a certain score. This, believe me, does not work.

How is the work we do in Geography different from other lessons?

The big difference with Geography lessons is that we are

encouraged to think for ourselves.

In Geography we are often involved with finding things out. We are always asked what we think, and why, and are generally expected to think for ourselves rather than being told what is right.

We usually know what we have to cover in the next few weeks and are allowed to work at our own pace. We can decide what to cover during the lesson and what to do for homework. For example, you might be doing coursework at home so you do less homework. Someone else might do some coursework during lesson time and do some notes for homework instead.

We discuss things in small groups, or sometimes as a class, things that are not understood thoroughly. By speaking to others, things that aren't clear are made more understandable.

We virtually always work in small groups and are allowed to help one another. Sometimes the teacher works with us and explains anything that we don't understand. This is much better, as you can ask questions that you wouldn't do if everyone else was listening.

We usually work in small groups and are always encouraged to talk about the work. Anything that you don't understand can be explained by a friend.

The teacher works with different groups in turn. He answers any problems and generally chats to us. He normally asks us questions to find out how much we understand.

We are constantly encouraged to look for key points and have been taught how to identify and extract the important information from books, graphs, etc. We are told to concentrate on important questions such as how? why? when? The teacher is always stressing the difference between describing and explaining.

We are never told to take notes or write anything down. We are encouraged to note down any key point or things that we might need to remember.

We were taught to make notes at the beginning and just write things down when we want.

Rough notes are always turned into neat notes. We are encouraged to keep these short and concentrate on key points and examples.

Notes can be written up in any way but most people draw some form of spider diagrams. Some people do mind-mapping. This was a technique that we were taught.

When I write notes twice I am more likely to remember them. Because we just write in key points there is less writing and we are more likely to remember it.

When I get home and read my rough notes I turn them into neat notes. This means that I have to think about the work again. Anything I do not really understand I look up in a book.

Geography is the only lesson where we were taught how to learn. We looked at the right and left brain and how important colour and visual images are. This is why most people write up their notes in colour and use diagrams and visual images. We were also taught how to revisit information. This means that we go over our diagrams after five minutes, one day, one week and one month. I find this really helps me to learn information and remember it.

At the end of each topic revision sheets or cards are written. We are encouraged to look at these regularly - a day after we do the work, a week after, a month after; this is called 'revisiting' and helps us remember.

I find that each piece of information has gone through my brain at least three times. Once in class, once when I am writing up my notes and once when I am making revision cards. This helps me learn it.

The approach the teacher uses is the 'friendly teacher approach'. He talks to us and advises us on how to tackle the work. Instead of threatening us with detentions he encourages us to learn.

We often work in small groups with the teacher. The relationship between pupil and teacher is more of a friendly one than a teacher-dominant one. We are treated as individuals rather than as a group.

Obviously the teacher explains Geography to us but he also helps us with other things like how much time to spend on our work and how to meet deadlines.

What are the advantages of working like this?

I find that I really understand the work rather than just writing things down because I am told to. If I don't understand I know that I can always ask.

Often I find that my friends can explain things to me in a way that I understand. I like working in small groups.

Although it is hard work, I find it more interesting to work things out for myself rather than just sit there and be told things. Normally I enjoy Geography and because of this I generally work harder.

The advantage is that we know exactly what we have got to cover and why we are doing things.

Because we have talked about how our brain works and how we learn, I know why I am doing things and how they are helping me.

I find I remember things better if I have had to work them out for myself. I also remember things better because the information has gone through my brain at least three times.

I like it when the teacher talks to us in small groups. I don't mind asking questions about things that I don't understand but I am too shy in front of the whole class.

It is good to work at your own pace. In other lessons I often have to wait for other people to catch up. Working in key points is much easier and means that we have fewer notes. Therefore we are more likely to remember them.

Using these techniques has helped me realise that we can't store large amounts of information for long periods but by doing things like revisiting we can keep reminding ourselves of the work.

What are the disadvantages of working like this?

Because I hadn't been taught like this before I found it quite hard at first. Other people who were used to this way of working were much better than I, and I was quite worried at first.

I would like to have worked like this lower down the school as some of my friends did. They said it was much easier working like this because they were used to it but I found it quite hard. I soon got used to it, however, although I still think that it would have been a good idea to have done this before.

Sometimes it is harder work than other subjects, although I don't really mind as I know that I am really learning and making progress.

I find other subjects quite boring compared with Geography and often get frustrated because I think we are wasting time.

I wish we could work like this in other subjects.

Past Pupils: Degree Student

The following evaluation was written by a former pupil who studied Geography to GCSE level at Balcarras School and is currently studying for a degree in the subject.

How were Geography lessons different from others?

*The lessons were far more inspiring and we definitely became
more motivated. Our interest was maintained through a form of
teaching that we could relate to. We, as individuals, became
more independent and we did not require the teacher's undivided
attention at all times but merely needed guidance with our tasks.
We never copied off the blackboard as in a lot of other lessons
but instead chose our own method of working around central
themes. Within our lessons we were encouraged to think for
ourselves, and we generated our own thoughts and feelings
rather than relying on teachers' dictation.*

How did we work?

*We worked within a system of note-taking by concentrating on
key words and points. This produced a framework to which we,
the students, could apply what we felt was important to our
learning. We adapted knowledge gathered from videos, textbooks, computer packages and audio-visual information to a
level we felt reached our own personal goals. We then
established different ways of presenting the data collected by the
use of diagrams, graphs and statistics. Homework was
generally re-writing notes. Our work was monitored regularly,
enabling any problems to be quickly identified without
disrupting our progress. Discussions within small groups were
encouraged and this improved class relations and enabled
individuals to improve their understanding of topics.*

Advantages of working within the system

*We gained independence, being responsible, in many ways, for
our learning. We worked at our own ability levels, covering
points we felt were important rather than covering aspects of the
subject we already had a sound knowledge of. The lessons were
always varied and far less monotonous than traditional ones,
and a more relaxed class atmosphere encouraged harder work
by the students.*

Disadvantages of working within this system

Personally, I feel there are few drawbacks to this learning system. Although more demand and responsibility is placed upon teachers to ensure learning, I feel that due to the variety and individuality of the work produced by the pupils their job becomes more interesting and more rewarding. After all, they are marking the pupils' own work and not merely their own dictation. I also feel that by introducing the scheme to other lessons, not only Geography, many benefits would be acknowledged and an increase in the popularity of school would be inevitable.

How did it prepare me for 'A' Level?

The progression from GCSE to 'A' Level was vast; however, due to our previous method of learning we were able to cope with the change. Note-taking techniques were essential, and although traditional dictation was administered it was up to the individual to read around the subjects to gain further knowledge. Again, an independent attitude was needed to use the available resources to greatest effect. Due to our previous experiences adapting to 'A' Level study was made considerably easier, although more detail was required.

Key concepts were another important issue, as all examination questions concentrated upon using words like 'describe', 'explain', 'why', 'how' and 'evaluate'. Previous understanding of these was essential in order to tackle such questions and build self-confidence. I believe the background knowledge and techniques received at GCSE stood us in good stead for the transition to 'A' Level.

How has it helped with my degree?

The whole concept of undergraduate education is based upon independent study. It is up to the individuals to select what they feel is important to their education. Lectures and tutorials are the only form of guidance available. Additional information is then obtained from other resources at the students' discretion. Note-taking is the key. Lectures are merely stimulus and it is impossible to handle all of what is being taught. Notes are the only option in securing an understanding of the topics covered.

Note-taking is an art, and by being taught this at an early stage of education it means more time can be spent enhancing knowledge.

Flexible learning also encourages students to consider self-assessment from an early age. This is important in higher education, in order to monitor progress, motivate the individual, establish personal organisation and introduce new methods of presentation. These are major themes and highlight in many ways what flexible learning is all about.

Key words and points still remain the most important part of learning and understanding Geography, particularly at degree level. You must be aware of such words as 'describe', 'explain', 'evaluate', 'how?' and 'why?' and use them accordingly within tutorial and examination essays. I believe, therefore, that my association with this form of teaching has led to my continuation of geographical study. I have no doubts that the initial background I received at GCSE was very effective and has helped me no end to gain independence and self-confidence, not only at university but in life in general.

First-year undergraduate

I was a pupil at Balcarras during the early stages of the development of flexible learning. Therefore, because I was previously taught under traditional methods, the conversion to flexible learning took place at a steady pace. However, at this early stage the characteristics of flexible learning could be clearly seen. Geography lessons were different from other subjects in a variety of ways. The main difference that I found was the relaxed atmosphere in which the class worked. This allowed me to work comfortably, which in turn resulted in more productive study. The lessons were enjoyable, although a high standard of work was expected.

It was in Geography that I learned the main fundamentals behind taking comprehensive notes and the importance of highlighting key points. I also learned to always ask myself the five main questions - what? where? why? how and when? We were expected to think for ourselves in Geography, rather than immediately asking the teacher for help when a problem emerged as I tended to do in other subjects. I was encouraged to use other resources for the solution first, and if the problem still existed I then sought help from the teacher.

As we became more accustomed to the format of flexible learning our individual contributions to the lessons increased.

We never had to experience dictation or copying from the blackboard, which were popular methods of teaching within other subjects. This enabled each lesson to be stimulating, whereas the boredom experienced in connection with dictation meant that one lesson merged into another. This made revision difficult for my other subjects.

During the latter stages of my study of Geography at Balcarras, the importance of groupwork increased. This allowed the teacher to work through any difficulties with us in small groups, rather than causing the whole class to cease working in order to listen to the problem. Thus, the pupils who didn't share the problem could continue with their study. Another advantage that I found from flexible learning was that those of a higher ability were encouraged to partake in further reading whilst those of slightly less ability were able to work at their required level of understanding. Because in the traditional teaching of my other subjects the brighter pupils were not stretched enough whilst the pupils of lower ability felt swamped, only the average pupils were properly catered for. The only disadvantage that I feel could result from flexible learning is the possibility that pupils could abuse the system. However, this should not occur if the student knows that his/her work is being regularly checked, which is part of the practice of flexible learning.

I feel that the learning methods which I experienced whilst working towards my GCSEs helped me adapt quickly to the differences found at 'A' Level. For example, through flexible learning I had been taught to think for myself and had developed self-motivation towards studying. I already knew that nobody was going to make me work and that much of my study was going to stem from background reading rather than from the classroom. The main reason that I chose to study Geography at 'A' Level was that I enjoyed the subject and understood it. I feel that this was as a result of the flexible learning that I experienced during my latter years at Balcarras. Flexible learning also allowed me to be prepared for university because of my ability to take comprehensive notes whilst highlighting the key points, all of which was learnt prior to GCSE. It has also made me more disciplined in self-study, which is an essential aspect of university.

How did Geography differ from other subjects?

Flexible learning made Geography much more enjoyable than many of the other subjects available. Because tasks were continually varied and were undertaken both individually and within groups, interest and enthusiasm was always present and always acted as a stimulus for hard work. As well as generally being more fun, learning in Geography emphasised the individual's effort rather than that of the teacher, with no use of dictation and rare use of copying from the blackboard. This helped develop the skills of individuals, and personally it has continued to help me with all of my subjects. Flexible learning enables the student to become more flexible in learning, to consider everything, and it also encourages the use of all resources and thus a more thorough approach to the tasks set.

Classes were generally quite active and often tasks took place outside the classroom with the introduction of fieldwork, which often enabled the theories learnt from books, television and the computer to become more life-like and logical. Such trips emphasised how learning should be fun and how certain subjects which may originally seem illogical become logical and how they affect all our lives.

Effectively, I found Geography to be one of the most organised subjects, because we were always aware of our personal aims, and this helped us all aim high and therefore work hard. Exam techniques were practised throughout, mark schemes were made openly available and revision notes were in practice from the start of the course. Such factors meant that ultimately our exams would not seem so foreign to us and again we were aware of our personal aims and, maybe, what we needed to improve ourselves. The importance of key words was emphasised in our learning and in exam questions, and were often a basis for our investigations, a process which proved valid at the time and remains so on a degree course.

What are the advantages of flexible learning?

I feel the main advantage of flexible learning is that it allows the individual to flourish. If a subject is enjoyable it increases the enthusiasm of pupils and they therefore work harder. Flexible learning thus produces better personal organisation, harder work and ultimately better results.

Personally I feel that flexible learning has been particularly advantageous not only to my Geography but to my own organisational skills when learning daily. Skills, such as note-taking, which have been learnt thoroughly during flexible learning, have proved important and are continually being built upon; key words are now automatically noted and either questioned or answered.

How flexible learning influenced my choice at 'A' Level

Flexible learning has been a major influence in both my choice to continue Geography at 'A' Level and degree level and in the way I work within the subject itself. I feel that it has acted as a very solid foundation both in knowledge and skills on which I have been able to build. The knowledge I gained has fed my enthusiasm and I have learnt through flexible learning essential skills, such as note-taking, key-words and the use of all resources. These, without a doubt, helped me in 'A' Level.

Even though more traditional teaching methods were adopted at 'A' Level, I feel that it has been the development of these foundation skills which has given me the confidence and capability to use my own judgement whilst undertaking different tasks, and I feel that it has definitely been a great aid in my continual learning.

Sixth form Teachers

Balcarras students wishing to go on to education 16+ have tended to enter the Sixth Form College in Cheltenham.

The following section is a submission from the Geography department at the college which has taken students onto 'A' Level courses from a number of schools, including Balcarras.

This section is a distillation of the views of members of the Geography department over the past six years. They result from INSET discussions, formal and informal departmental meetings and, most importantly, interactions with students. At this point, I would like emphasise that we do not think or refer to students by their previous school. Where the students come from makes no difference to us, but we feel that trends do emerge and I use the term 'Balcarras students' out of convenience.

1) Induction

(a)   The department has traditionally run an induction course at the beginning of the 'A' Level course concentrating on note-taking, key ideas, command words, using resources, etc.

(b)   We have found Balcarras students very receptive to the concept of induction prior to the course and they have proved to be adept at working with materials.

2) Note-taking

Any student embarking on an 'A' Level course is liable to find this difficult. We have found that Balcarras students have a clearer idea of the essentials of the process. This applies both in and out of class.

3) *Written work*

We find that Balcarras students are:

(a) *more punctual*

(b) *better organised*

(c) *more able to produce relevant answers.*

4) *Coursework*

(a) *Our major experience with 'A' Level coursework has been the individual study (worth 28%). This requires the student to submit a form to the moderator showing:*

    i.   *the title*

    ii. *the route to enquiry - a series of key questions which guide the student through the project*

    iii. *statistical and cartographic methods appropriate to the study.*

(b) *In general we find Balcarras students are more effective in a number of areas:*

    i.   *they show initiative in selecting the topic*

    ii. *they are markedly better at designing the route to enquiry/key questions*

    iii. *they often seem to have a clearer idea of how and where the project is going.*

5) *Resources*

The department has a range of resources (including human) available to students. Balcarras students tend to be better at:

(a) *ascertaining what is available*

(b) *using the resources as information sources*

(c) *applying the information from the resources in a logical manner.*

6) Overall

The department has been impressed with the academic and social qualities of the students from Balcarras. Generalisations are by their nature not universally applicable, but we have found the students to be:

   (a)   well motivated

   (b)   capable of independent work

   (c)   capable of using their initiative

   (d)   responsive to new/challenging situations

   (e)   not frightened to ask for help.

Parents' Perceptions

Inevitably, the parents of pupils who were working in this manner became aware that the way in which their children were studying Geography was significantly different from the way in which they were being educated in other curriculum areas. Many parents took a great deal of interest in the concept of flexible learning and the progress that their children were making. During discussions at Parents' Evenings numerous parents reported that children were working harder and for longer periods on Geography and were talking about their learning with increased enthusiasm. Such positive parental feedback has been most encouraging. Although such evidence is largely subjective and cannot be quantified, comments such as, 'My son has been inspired to learn,' are of significance. Consequently, a number of parents were requested to commit their perceptions of flexible learning to paper and it is their responses that are summarised below:

She certainly has worked very hard and probably harder than if conventionally taught.

My daughter has certainly worked hard, but, more importantly, has worked with a great deal of enthusiasm. There is a great sense of pride in the things she does.

They seem to put more effort into their work.

This form of teaching encourages students to undertake their own research. It encourages initiative and pays dividends in other ways by sharpening the students' skills in collating and prioritising information.

He adopts his own style when preparing work and therefore chooses the methods that please him. This makes the work more satisfying as he is interpreting it rather than being dictated to.

They don't seem to regard it as work, more as a hobby.

They are in control of what they do and are not limited by the teacher.

She likes to express herself creatively and this form of teaching allows her to be more open-minded in her presentation and content.

He is learning how to improve his research skills and as he gets more involved in his work he continues to improve.

A vast amount of enjoyment and interest is gained through flexible learning.

He definitely enjoys this subject. He seems far more interested in it than he was when the traditional teaching methods were used.

Geography has always been high on her list of subjects but this method of learning has underlined and enhanced this.

He often talks about what he is learning or doing and seems very enthusiastic about it.

She does talk a great deal about flexible learning and is very keen to get us involved in it too.

She undoubtedly has a more profound grasp of this subject and speaks more confidently on it than on any other subject in the curriculum.

I think it is a good method of learning and generally enables him to remember the facts better as he has researched it himself and written notes.

They do gain confidence and experience with each unit and satisfaction from their achievements.

I wish this had been at my school when I was a child.

It is with some envy that I watch her work in this way. I am grateful that she has been given the opportunity.

4

Evaluation of Pupil Outcomes

EVALUATION OF PUPIL OUTCOMES

There is little doubt that young people enjoy working in the ways described in Chapter 2. The overwhelming majority of pupils of all ages report greater enjoyment, increased motivation and additional effort as a direct consequence of using flexible learning methods. Many also recognise that this style of work enhances their studies in other curriculum areas, contributes to their personal development and effectively prepares them for further academic study after leaving school.

This consistent message, however, is not, by itself, sufficient. A number of parties - colleagues, governors, parents and pupils - will be concerned with the effects that flexible learning has on attainment levels. It is perfectly legitimate for them to enquire whether this form of learning is more effective than the traditional forms of classroom experiences it replaces.

Judging the influence of a particular learning style on attainment is undoubtedly more difficult than ascertaining pupils' perceptions and for this reason it is often neglected when evaluating curriculum developments. It is accepted that a multitude of factors will influence pupil attainment and that any attempt to isolate the impact of the teaching style employed will not only be fraught with difficulties but will also be largely context-specific. This should not, however, prevent some form of attainment analysis taking place.

In an attempt to measure the effect that flexible learning had upon attainment in Geography at Balcarras School, four investigations were conducted:

- Year 9 controlled experiment
- GCSE examination results
- GCSE results related to VRQ
- GCSE coursework marks.

Year 9 Controlled Experiment

Two groups of Year 9 pupils studied the topic of Japan for a six-week period during the autumn term of 1992. One group approached its work along the flexible learning lines described earlier, negotiating an individual action plan from a study guide, while the other group was taught in a more traditional manner with the teacher using the study guide only as a scheme of work.

All of the pupils were aware that at the end of the module that they would be tested, and were encouraged to prepare thoroughly. They were not informed, however, that they would be re-tested six weeks later in an attempt to assess genuine understanding and to establish how much information had been 'lost' during the period.

The content and nature of the test was agreed upon by both teachers and included a range of questions from straightforward recall (e.g. 'What is the population of Japan?') to questions that required an extended answer (e.g. 'Explain in as much detail as you can why Japan has developed into such a successful industrial nation'). The two groups in question were parallel top sets and regarded as similar in ability by the school. This is illustrated when VRQ at intake is considered. The average VRQ for the flexible learning group was 108.05 compared to an average of 107.1 for the group taught in a more traditional style.

The results revealed the following points:

- The flexible learning group scored higher on both tests.

- The flexible learning group scored higher in the re-test, after a gap of six weeks, than the traditional group scored on the first test.

- The loss in performance was significantly less (2.9 marks or 12%) in the flexible learning group than in the traditional group (5.74 marks or 30%).

- The highest mark in the flexible learning group was 6 marks higher than the top score in the traditional group for the first test and 13 marks higher for the second.

- The lowest mark for the flexible learning group was 6 marks higher than the lowest score in the traditional group for the first test and 8 marks higher for the second.

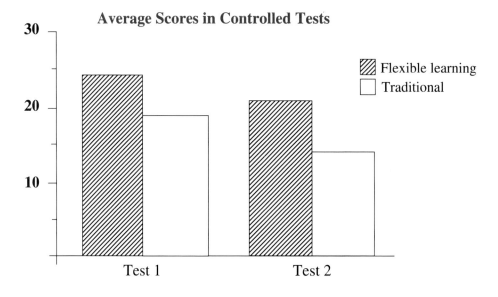

Average Scores in Controlled Tests

Flexible learning VRQ 108.5	Test One	Test Two
Highest score Lowest score	34 15	31 13
Average score	**24.00**	**21.1**

Drop in performance: 2.9 marks or 12%

Traditional learning VRQ 107.1	Test One	Test Two
Highest score Lowest score	28 9	18 5
Average score	**19.04**	**13.3**

Drop in performance: 5.74 marks or 30%

GCSE Examination Results

Although many would agree that raw examination results are not the only indicator of the quality of educational provision, senior managers, governors and parents have a right to ask how a new approach, particularly one that is so significantly different from the norm, affects pupil performance in public examinations. GCSE examination results are undoubtedly an important performance indicator. The publication of league tables of results will mean that such indicators become even more significant.

Balcarras School is an 11-16 mixed comprehensive. However, the presence of a selective grammar school in the town ensures that the children of high academic ability are 'filtered off'. Formerly a secondary modern institution, it was not until 1991 that the first comprehensive intake sat GCSE examinations at Balcarras.

The following examination result analysis is based upon children sitting the Southern Examination Group GCSE examination (syllabus A2) in Geography.

As explained in Chapter 1, each year a proportion of the pupils were educated along traditional lines, whilst flexible learning methods were employed to deliver the syllabus to selected groups.

Pupils were not setted or grouped by ability. The groups were mixed ability and ranged from grade A candidates to grade G. In the vast majority of cases pupils were placed in a group as a result of their previous experiences in Geography. A flexible learning approach was adopted with pupils who had previously experienced this style of learning, while children who were used to more traditional methods continued to be educated in this way.

The analysis is intended to be a comparison of the relative effectiveness of teaching styles and was conducted over a four-year period (1989-92) in an attempt to minimise possible distortions.

Section One

The grades obtained by children experiencing the two approaches are reproduced in Table I. Information is given for individual years, followed by a four-year summary.

1992 (comprehensive intake)

	A	B	C	D	E	F	G	U	No.A-C	%A-C
Traditional learning	3	5	5	5	2	1	1	-	13	59
Flexible learning	9	17	15	4	3	-	-	-	41	85

1991 (1st comprehensive intake)

	A	B	C	D	E	F	G	U	No.A-C	%A-C
Traditional learning	1	5	9	8	5	6	4	1	15	38
Flexible learning	5	5	5	4	4	1	0	0	15	63

1990 (secondary modern intake)

	A	B	C	D	E	F	G	U	No.A-C	%A-C
Traditional learning	0	4	5	10	9	3	2	2	9	25
Flexible learning	5	6	4	3	1	0	0	0	15	78

1989 (secondary modern intake)

	A	B	C	D	E	F	G	U	No.A-C	%A-C
Traditional learning	0	1	2	4	2	2	4	3	3	16
Flexible learning	4	8	8	11	5	9	1	2	20	41

Table I

This graph shows the GCSE grades obtained by Geography candidates in the period 1989-92 using traditional and flexible learning techniques:

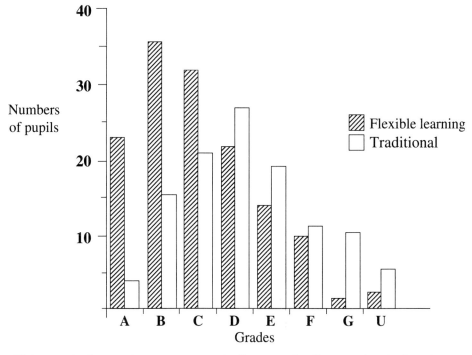

This graph shows the percentage A-C passes in Geography during the period 1989-92 using traditional and flexible learning techniques:

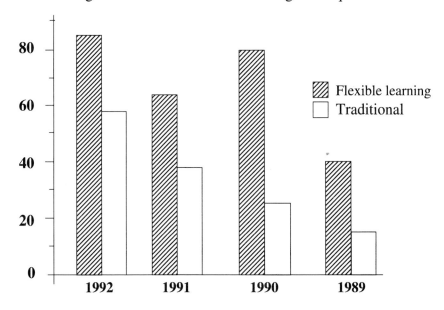

Section Two

It should be stressed, at this point, that Balcarras School enjoys a deserved reputation for academic achievement, and the excellent 1992 figures of 52% with 5 or more A-C passes is even more commendable when one takes into consideration the presence of a selective grammar school in the town which denies Balcarras access to many of the more able local young people.

Without a doubt, high-quality teaching permeates the school. This, therefore, is not a comparison between flexible learning and poor-quality traditional teaching. Nor is it intended to be a reflection upon the abilities of individuals. As far as possible it is intended to be a comparison between teaching and learning styles, even though the difficulty in isolating the teaching style from the teacher has already been acknowledged.

Flexible learning has been compared with other styles of teaching which, although labelled for convenience 'traditional', vary significantly from classroom to classroom. The comparison has been made with the approaches adopted by around 30 other teachers, including many experienced colleagues of proven ability, and still flexible learning is shown in a favourable light.

Although these raw data are revealing, cynics may well argue that one group, despite efforts to ensure mixed-ability groups of roughly equal ability, was more able than the other and contained more pupils capable of high grades.

It would certainly appear that the flexible learning group were more highly motivated and worked harder. Indeed, I would claim that a greater interest and dedication to working generated by the flexible learning approach is one of the major plus points of these approaches.

However, in order to minimise any possible variations between the groups it was decided to carry out a second analysis. This involved comparing the grade that a pupil obtained for Geography with the grades that he/she achieved in all other subjects. As Geography was initially the only department to have formally adopted the flexible learning approach, this would be an accurate comparison of flexible learning with the more traditional approaches adopted in other curriculum areas.

To do this, grades were given a numeric value; grade A = 8, grade B = 7, down to U, which was awarded 1 mark. Pupils' grades in Geography could then be compared with their average performance.

Results are also given for pupils who studied Geography in a traditional fashion. It is clear that pupils are not gaining higher grades because of the nature of the subject or the relative difficulty of the examination. It is the style in which they have studied that is proving to be more effective for the vast majority of pupils.

Below is a comparison of GCSE grades obtained using flexible learning in Geography with other, more traditional styles.

	Pupils gaining a higher grade for Geography than their average grade	Pupils gaining a lower grade for Geography than their average grade
1992		
Flexible learning	68%	27%
Traditional	43%	47%
1991		
Flexible learning	58%	33%
Traditional	25%	69%
1990		
Flexible learning	63%	21%
Traditional	11%	88%
1989		
Flexible learning	62%	29%
Traditional	33%	66%
4 Year summary		
Flexible learning	63%	27%
Traditional	28%	67%

NB   i.   Pupils whose grade for Geography was equal to their average grade are not recorded in this analysis.

        ii.   Results for Modern Languages were excluded after the department also adopted flexible learning techniques in the delivery of GCSE.

        iii.   1990/91 figures were calculated before all Science scripts were re-marked.

This graph shows the performance of pupils in GCSE using both flexible learning and traditional teaching approaches, in comparison with their performance in other subjects:

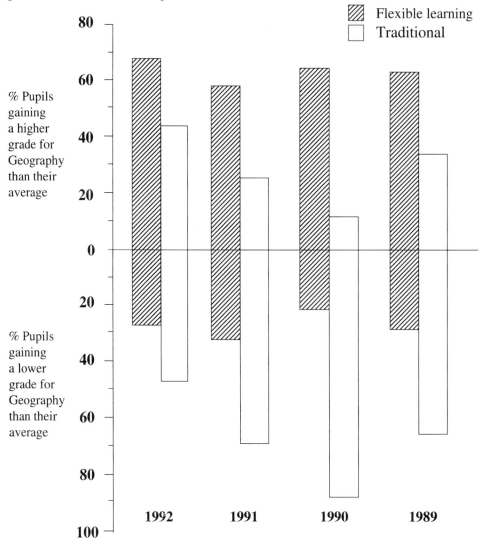

Speculation that this might be the result of an easier examination was dispelled when one considers that pupils studying Geography along more traditional lines averaged 0.5 (half a grade) lower for Geography than for their other subjects over the four-year period studied.

A full breakdown of the four years is as follows:

	Average Geography grade compared to average GCSE grade
1992 Flexible learning Traditional	0.48 Higher 0.10 Lower
1991 Flexible learning Traditional	0.25 Higher 0.50 Lower
1990 Flexible learning Traditional	0.20 Higher 0.60 Lower
1989 Flexible learning Traditional	0.30 Higher 0.40 Lower

Over the four-year period, pupils who had study along flexible learning lines averaged 0.31 (which is the equivalent to a third of a grade) higher for Geography than for their other subjects.

GCSE Examination Results Related to VRQ at Intake

Balcarras School 1991
Procedure

Pupils are divided into four categories based on VRQ at intake. The four categories are as follows:

- 85 and below
- 101 - 115
- 16 - 100
- 116 and above

GCSE grades are awarded a value. A=8, B=7......., U=1.

The average grade for pupils sitting an examination in each category can be calculated.

i.   Science results are not included in the calculation as they were subject to an appeal.

ii. A very small number of children who moved to the school during their five years of secondary education had no recorded VRQ score and were omitted from this study.

iii. Figures are rounded down to one decimal place.

The following are the average grade for Balcarras School (1991) in *all subjects* except Geography and Science.

VRQ	School Average	Geography Flexible learning	Geography Traditional
85 or below	4.1	No candidates	4.0
86 - 100	4.5	4.5	3.8
101 - 115	5.6	6.5	5.3
116 or above	6.1	7.0	6.2

The perception that flexible learning has greater benefit for more able students is largely confirmed by this analysis. Brighter pupils are not held back as they are in whole-class situations; instead they are able to progress at a pace and to a depth more suited to their ability and consequently are fully stretched. The difference in average grades is most significant, therefore, in pupils with a VRQ score of 101 and above.

GCSE Coursework

There was a noticeable difference in the way in which the groups who were following a flexible learning approach to GCSE geography approached their coursework. Within the flexible learning groups, individual pupils take a substantial amount of responsibility for their coursework, basing their enquiry around negotiated action plans and regular tutorial support. The procedure adopted is outlined as follows:

- Pupils are introduced to the idea of coursework and issued with the pink booklet, 'GCSE Geography - A Coursework Guide'. Other publications dealing with GCSE coursework are recommended and include examples of possible titles. (See Appendix F.)

- By now pupils will have indentified which aspect of Geography they wish to study, e.g. rivers, settlement, agriculture, etc. They will now refer to a specific study guide about their chosen topic. Within the department there are Network Educational Press study guides and ones that have been written by members of staff.

- Candidates now complete a first draft of their individual action plans.

- Pupils then discuss their ideas with their teacher. It is during this discussion that the member of staff can ensure that the pupils are proposing a study that is suitable for their levels of ability. As a result of this crucial discussion, the action plan is confirmed and completed and a schedule decided upon.

- Pupils can then carry out investigations in accordance with the agreed plan.

- Regular tutorials are arranged with the teacher so that a check can be kept on the progress of the enquiry. During these tutorials any problems can be ironed out and suggestions can be made for improvements. In addition to these planned tutorials, pupils can request a meeting at any time if they need any extra guidance. During tutorials candidates are encouraged to assess their own work using the prompts 'Things I was pleased with' and 'Things I could have improved'.

An analysis of the marks obtained by pupils adopting this procedure compared to candidates who experienced a less structured approach to their enquiry show a significant difference in outcomes. The analysis was conducted over a four-year period (maximum mark 40).

SEG GCSE Geography coursework (maximum 40)

		Flexible learning	Traditional
1992	Highest score	38	38
	Lowest score	20	12
	Average	30	25
1991	Highest score	38	33
	Lowest score	16	7
	Average	28.5	20.3
1990	Highest score	38	29
	Lowest score	22	7
	Average	31.5	16.3
1989	Highest score	33	26
	Lowest score	6	2
	Average	19.5	12.8
	4-year average	**27.3**	**18.6**

A look at the number of pupils gaining a mark of 30 or higher is of significance:

		Flexible learning	Traditional
1992	Number over 30	26	7
	As a % of candidates	55%	30%
1991	Number over 30	10	5
	As a % of candidates	41.6%	12.8%
1990	Number over 30	13	0
	As a % of candidates	68.4%	0
1989	Number over 30	6	0
	As a % of candidates	12.5%	0
Total	Number over 30	29	5
	As a % of candidates	31.8%	5.4%
	4-year average	**55**	**12**
		44%	**10.7%**

GCSE coursework lends itself to a flexible learning approach, and an analysis of the coursework marks reveals that the methods benefit pupils at both ends of the ability spectrum. More specifically:

i. a flexible learning approach, and the associated tutorial support, ensures that pupils do not 'slip through the net' and end up with very low marks;

ii. a flexible learning approach helps candidates of high ability gain significantly higher marks (over 30).

Conclusion

Firm conclusions have largely been avoided as the figures speak for themselves. While sceptics may claim that such data can be skewed by any number of factors, five points are worth highlighting:

- The examination results and other raw data are a presentation of the facts. Individuals are left to interpret them and attach significance for themselves.

- Although there are factors which can distort an analysis of this nature, it should be noted that the statistics were gleaned from more than 120 candidates, for a four-year period in a range of over a dozen subjects involving around 30 teachers.

- Governors and parents have every right to request such data to enable them to evaluate the effectiveness of a new initiative for themselves.

- It is interesting to speculate on the response from all interested parties if the results had been inverted. Any new teaching style that was proved to be less effective than the one it was intended to replace would quickly wither and die.

- Taken in isolation, the results from each individual analysis can be questioned and explained away by a variety of factors. However, when all the evidence is accumulated and gives a consistent message, that message is considerably strengthened and forms a convincing argument.

5

Final Thoughts

Increase in Pupil Motivation
Improvement in Pupil Behaviour
Increase in Pupil Attainment
Increase in Pupil Responsibility
Effective Differentiation
Pupil Assessment
Major Implications
The Future

FINAL THOUGHTS

The picture would be incomplete without an analysis of flexible learning methods from the perspective of the classroom teacher. I would highlight the following points as being the main outcomes of working in this way:

- there is a dramatic increase in pupil motivation
- it improves pupil behaviour
- there is a significant increase in pupil attainment and an all-round raising of standards
- pupils take an increasing amount of responsibility for their learning
- work is effectively differentiated
- pupil assessment is more effective.

Increase in Pupil Motivation

There is no doubt that pupils enjoy working in this style. Pupils of all ages and abilities report an increase in motivation, and consequently children are working harder and for longer periods than would normally be the case. This alone would have a significant effect on outcomes, but when coupled with learning styles that promote deeper and genuine understanding, performance is significantly improved. In short, pupils work harder and for longer on more effective learning activities.

I would also add that during this time of upheaval and turmoil in the world of education, when excessive and extraordinary demands are greatly reducing teacher morale, witnessing so many young people respond in such an enthusiastic and positive manner to this learning environment has been a constant source of satisfaction and stimulation. Although anecdotal evidence is largely subjective and cannot be quantified, the positive parental feedback and reports of children being 'inspired to learn' have been extremely encouraging.

Improvement in Pupil Behaviour

The Committee of Enquiry on pupil behaviour chaired by Lord Elton reported in 1989 that many children who behave badly in school are those whose self-esteem is threatened by failure.

(Discipline in School, Report of the Committee of Enquiry chaired by Lord Elton, HMSO 1989)

The best way to raise self-esteem among young people is to provide for them. There is no doubt in my mind that young people who are succeeding enjoy their work more, and behave better. This cycle is self-perpetuating.

Increase in Pupil Attainment

Although the evidence presented may well be disputed by some, there is no doubt in my mind that standards are raised and pupils' attainment is significantly higher when teaching and learning is conducted within the spirit and framework of flexible learning. The fact that isolating the impact of a particular teaching style to measure its effectiveness is exceptionally difficult is not disputed, but it is equally apparent that the accumulation of many and varied pieces of evidence is beginning to form a strong and consistent argument.

I regularly receive work of a higher standard than I would have expected prior to the flexible learning developments, and the result of the attainment analysis in Chapter 4 merely confirms what I had long suspected prior to this pilot study.

The GCSE results and the Year 9 controlled experiment are illuminating and, to my mind, offer convincing, if not conclusive, evidence that flexible learning strategies influence outcomes and raise pupil attainment. They are, of course, a presentation of the facts and individuals are left to interpret them for themselves, but whether received positively or with scepticism, they cannot be ignored.

Increase in Pupil Responsibity

The benefits of flexible learning are not confined to academic achievement. Pupils develop their self-confidence and quickly mature as a direct result of allowing them to take a greater responsibility for their progress. This is not confined to Geography. A noticeable spill-on effect into other curriculum areas and a number of reports from parents suggest that children have become noticeably more independent at home.

The pupils quickly develop a clear insight into how their activities help them to learn and then quickly reject any form of copying or reproducing information as being relatively ineffective. Personal organisation skills improve as pupils learn to allocate their time, including homework and conduct investigations and research for information as part of normal classroom practices. Groupwork skills and personal relationships are enhanced as the nature of the work brings about increased respect for, and reliance on, one another. Social skills are significantly developed and an atmosphere of cooperation and friendliness exists in the classroom, with bickering and discipline problems greatly reduced.

A genuine interest in, and commitment to, learning is apparent as pupils respond positively to the trust that is shown in them and to the opportunities that they are given.

Effective Differentiation

Achieving real differentiation is possibly the most satisfying aspect of the flexible learning approach as individual needs are catered for more effectively than ever before. Pupils are working on individual tasks at their own best pace for the vast majority of the time, and consequently far greater progress is made than would normally be expected. Although this is true for all pupils, it is most noticeable that the very able pupils are stretched more than in whole-class situations. One of the most dramatic examples of this was successfully working with three Year 8 pupils on a concept normally introduced at 'A' Level.

Although the profession has long been conscious of the need to cater for gifted children, time demands and the constraints of whole-class teaching have meant that the best intentions have not always been as effectively carried out as they might have been. Flexible learning undoubtedly raises both pupil and teacher expectations and provides a structure and procedure that enables differentiation to be a central feature of all lessons.

Pupil Assessment

The way in which flexible learning releases the teacher from whole-class responsibility and the daily administrative chores enables them to work intensively with small groups of pupils in tutorial situations. Much of this time will be devoted to assessment, either formally or informally, and thus assessment becomes an integral component of normal lessons. Talking to small groups of pupils rather than the whole class means:

- the depth and pace of exposition can be geared more closely to the needs of the group.

- pupils are far more likely to ask questions and become involved in discussion in a small group situation. Even the very shy pupils become reasonably talkative as their confidence improves with the increased security offered by small numbers.

- the teacher can quickly assess if everyone has fully grasped a particular point, and, if any misunderstandings exist, they can be corrected. This is not possible when dealing with an entire class simply because of the numbers involved.

- the teacher gets to know individual pupils more quickly and to a far greater depth, and personal relationships are enhanced as a result.

The second key feature of assessment within flexible learning is that the individual child is involved in the procedure. Pupils are encouraged to assess their work, not because they have to but because it is worthwhile and will help them improve. Involving pupils in the assessment process not only helps them to understand what is required of them and what is being assessed but leads to a greater acceptance and recognition of any areas that they could improve. Consequently, any individual learning difficulties are fully understood by both teacher and pupil and can be addressed through negotiated target-setting far more effectively than before.

Major Implications

Experience suggests that there are five major implications of working in this style:

- *Induction*
- *Classoom management*
- *Resources*
- *Study guides*
- *Tutorials.*

Induction

It is unrealistic to expect pupils to be comfortable and successful working in this style overnight. A gradual switch to this way of working can often be beneficial and effective and, when possible, should begin at an early age. If pupils are going to be successful independent learners they need to be introduced to the necessary skills beforehand, and to this end the preparation that children receive during Year 7 is crucial.

Classroom management

The classroom needs to be organised and managed so that teachers are able to mix whole-class, group and independent work as required. Pupils must be able to collect and retrieve resources without involving the teacher, and furniture arrangement must therefore allow movement.

Resources

Resources are critical. Not only are large amounts required, but pupils need open access to them and need to be aware of what is available. The departmental resources catalogue, which was compiled by pupils, is an invaluable aid in this respect, and so is the library resource centre.

Study guides

Study guides are invaluable. They enable teachers to share with pupils the learning targets and they act as a scheme for work, giving pupils clear understanding of what topics and skills they will be covering. Study guides give guidance on resources and provide stimulus and ideas for pupils, helping them to set clear and worthwhile personal targets. They can also act as an agenda for tutorials.

Tutorials

Tutorials are the key to the success of flexible learning. They must be planned, regular and held without interruption. They are vital opportunities for the teacher to ensure that pupils are engaged in suitable tasks, to monitor progress and to assess understanding. In addition, they provide regular contact, support and encouragement for all pupils, thus ensuring that no one becomes isolated or de-motivated.

One of the main barriers that prevents people from adopting a flexible learning approach is the fear that the system is open to abuse by poorly motivated children who settle for an easy ride. Although this has not been my experience, it is prudent to be conscious of the possibility and to take steps to ensure that this does not happen. Immediately it should be pointed out that the teacher is still in control of the classroom and sets standards of acceptable behaviour and effort and is still in a position to encourage and cajole as required. Thus what is unacceptable in a traditional classroom is equally unacceptable in a flexible learning setting. More specifically, the following features of flexible learning minimise the potential for abusing the system.

- *Log books.* These are monitored on a weekly basis and a constant check can be maintained on every pupil. Pupils who are not working or have failed to complete homework tasks can quickly be detected and dealt with.

- *Deadlines.* The need to meet deadlines and to cover clearly stated tasks on an action plan encourages the pupils to keep up to date with their work and to tick off activities as they complete them.

- *Motivation.* This is generally high, and consequently pupils are less likely to settle for an easy ride. There is no question that classroom control and discipline significantly improve as a direct result of working in this way.

Flexible learning is not a laid-back, easy alternative to schooling, and a relaxed atmosphere should not be confused with a less than challenging approach. It is not the 'death by a worksheet' approach popular in the 70s. When executed well, flexible learning is quite the opposite as it provides a formal and coherent structure that sets high standards and has high expectations. No one can argue with the current desire to raise standards in education, but interestingly there have been few, arguably no, pragmatic suggestions about how this might be done. The evidence to date, however, indicates that flexible learning provides an enjoyable yet rigorous approach to learning that does indeed significantly affect pupil outcomes. It is not an abdication of professional responsibility and the teacher in the role of subject expert is not lost. Instead, the impact of teacher exposition is enhanced by its sparing and selective use and by reducing the pupil audience from whole classes to small groups.

It is also important not to see flexible learning as yet another initiative that overworked teachers have to get to grips with. It is not another problem; rather, it is a solution to many of the problems that the profession currently faces. How can the National Curriculum be delivered to ensure effective differentiation and progression? How can assessment be conducted as part of normal lessons? How can youngsters be motivated and engaged? These are all questions that may be answered by flexible learning. Currently, schools and teachers are overwhelmed with having to respond to numerous and varying demands. They are having to respond to these demands at a time when reductions in spending can result in a shortage of resources and possible increases in class size. Flexible learning should be considered not only because it offers solutions to many problems, but also because it is an effective approach to teaching and learning.

Initially it is undeniably hard work for the teacher. It takes time for children to become accustomed to working in this style, and large reservoirs of energy are required to set up the system. Time is also required to prepare and write study guides, although this would be no more than normal preparation time. (Published study guides are available from Network Educational Press, details at the end of the book.) The initial hard work, however, is undoubtdly a worthwhile investment. When the system is understood and accepted by the pupils, the demands on teachers are significantly reduced as they are largely freed from trivial, yet time-consuming administrative tasks and are able to devote their attention to helping pupils to learn.

Few would argue that schools should be preparing young people for adult life and for the very different employment demands of the twenty-first century, and it was therefore interesting to note the similarities between the flexible learning framework and the Honda work structure, especially as they had been discovered, identified and highlighted by a Year 9 pupil as part of her work on Japan!

The National Curriculum and Training Targets, which aim to have 50% of young people at NVQ level III (or equivalent) by the year 2000, cites as one of its objectives:

> Education and training provision to develop self-reliance, flexibility and breadth.

In a similar way, few would dispute the aims of Balcarras, and many other schools, which include reference to

> assisting every pupil to develop their abilities to the full, to assist pupils to acquire knowledge and skills relevant to adult life and employment in a fast-changing world, to stimulate the curiosity and the imagination of pupils, to encourage them to take responsibility for themselves and their activities and to help pupils develop lively, enquiring minds.

While applauding the motives, I would seriously question whether these aims can be fully met in a traditional, whole-class setting and would present flexible learning as an effective alternative.

Flexible learning is effective. It was always desirable and worthwhile but now it would appear to be a necessary response to many of the recent developments in education. Ultimately, whatever is happening in the world outside their classrooms, teachers are still required to shut the door and engage with their pupils in learning activities, remembering that each pupil is an individual with unique and specific needs. Any approach that can cater for those individual needs, while proving enjoyable and raising standards, is surely worthy of lengthy consideration.

The Future

Pupil response to flexible learning and the impact and implications of the National Curriculum have prompted the Geography department to adopt the methodology *en bloc*. A standard approach to teaching in Years 7 and 8 has been developed based upon internally produced study guides which individual department members write in turn.

The effective spread of flexible learning across the department, and in particular the academic tutoring aspect of it, has been speeded up and enhanced by a recent team-teaching initiative. The involved department members giving up one non-contract period a week in order to team-teach with a colleague. Not only therefore are teachers witnessing good practice, but they are also providing constructive feedback and mutual support for one another.

Inevitably, those developments have not been confined to the Geography department and a number of teachers in a variety of curriculum areas have expressed an interest and become involved in teaching in a flexible learning manner. All indications are that this will continue, with a team-teaching scheme based on the Geography department model likely to be implemented in the near future.

Appendix A

Example of a Year 8 action plan

(See Chapter 2 page 28)

Balcarras School

FLEXIBLE LEARNING PROJECT

ACTION PLAN

NAME GREER COUNSELL   TG 2G1   DATE 4/6/91

UNIT DEVELOPMENT.

CONTENT DEVELOPING COUNTRIES — WHAT ARE THEY?
ECONOMIC INDICATORS? — WHICH ARE THEY?
RELATIONSHIPS BETWEEN VARIABLES   WHERE ARE THEY? (GLOBAL PATTERN).
SPEARMAN RANK CORRELATION   THEY? (GLOBAL PATTERN).
TEST.   WHICH ARE CONNECTED?
WHY ARE THEY CONNECTED?
ARE THE CONNECTIONS STRONG?

RESOURCE
DEVELOPMENT DATA SEARCH (COMPUTER PACKAGE)
ATLAS
DEVELOPMENT IN THE THIRD WORLD (BOOK BY MICHAEL MORRISH)
Pg 14.

PRESENTATION
1. WORLD MAP — DESTINATION OF DEVELOPED + DEVELOPING COUNTRIES
2. SCATTERGRAPH TO SHOW RELATIONSHIPS   (GLOBAL PATTERN).
   BETWEEN VARIABLES.
3. A4 PROJECT — IDENTIFICATION OF KEY POINTS.

TIMESCALE
1. INITIAL RESEARCH - 1 WEEK.
2. DEVELOPMENT DATA SEARCH - 1 WEEK
3. TESTING RELATIONSHIPS - 2 WEEKS.   } 5 WEEKS
4. CONCLUSION + WRITING UP PROJECT - 1 WEEK

AIM
MY AIM IS TO GAIN A BETTER UNDERSTANDING ABOUT THE
VARIATIONS IN THE LEVEL OF DEVELOPMENT BETWEEN
DIFFERENT COUNTRIES.

DEADLINE   **SIGNED PUPIL** Greer Counsell
9TH JULY.   **TEACHER** NSHughes

Appendix B
Page 2 of the Balcarras step by step guide to writing action plans
(See Chapter 2 page 28)

STEP 1

Getting Started

The first thing that you need to do is find out what
RESOURCES are available to you.

WHAT ARE RESOURCES?

Atlases
Textbooks
Videos
Audio Tapes
Software
Filmstrips
Photographs
Maps
People

CAN YOU THINK OF ANY OTHERS?

WHERE DO I LOOK?

Geography Resource Catalogue

Resources held in the Department

Library Resource Centre
  - ask the Librarian
  - wordsearch
  - browse through books

Public Library

Council Offices

At Home

CAN YOU THINK OF ANYWHERE ELSE TO LOOK?

Page 3 of the Balcarras step by step
guide to writing action plans

Getting an Overview

Have a quick look at the resources you have collected.
Try and build up a picture in your mind about the topic you are studying - this is called an **OVERVIEW.**

Usually a good way of getting an overview is to watch a video.

- REMEMBER TO TAKE NOTES!

Talk in your groups about what you find interesting and what you might like to study. (YOU MAY GET SOME IDEAS FROM YOUR RESOURCES)

Decide which resources will be useful.
- is the resource
  * up to date?
  * in colour?
  * too hard?
  * too easy?

Page 4 of the Balcarras step by step
guide to writing action plans

 STEP 3

Write a rough action plan

By now you will have a picture in your mind of what you are studying and a good idea of the resources that are available to you.

The next step is to write a rough version of your action plan.

This can be done on your own or in small groups.
It is often a good idea to discuss your plans in groups as this helps you clarify your ideas.

This is the time to think about the **KEY WORDS ....**

84

Page 5 of the Balcarras step by step
guide to writing action plans

 STEP 4

The key words

As a geographer you will need to be able to **DESCRIBE** and **EXPLAIN**.

Keep asking yourself the question **WHY?**

As soon as you start answering the question why you are **EXPLAINING**.

DESCRIBE

Where is it?
How big/small is it?
What colour is it?
How hot/cold is it?
When did it happen?
What pattern does it make?

WHY?

EXPLAIN

Why is it there?
Why is it that size?
Why is it that colour?
Why is it that hot/cold?
Why did it happen then?
Why does it make that pattern?

Remember one of the first things you need to know as a Geographer is **WHERE** something is. ie. the **LOCATION**

Appendix C
Example of a teacher-prepared Balcarras study guide
(See Chapter 2 page 28)

Development

What is development?

This unit is based around the computer package **Devlopment Data Search**. When you have completed your work you should:

➤ *be able to recognise the characteristics of a developed and a developing nation*

➤ *understand what is meant by development*

➤ *understand what factors indicate the level of development*

➤ *have identified a global pattern of development*

You may use the computer package and any other resources any way you wish, although here are some suggestions:

Look at the list of Economic Variables

➤ *think about/discuss the importance of each one*

➤ *why do you think they indicate development?*

Use Top Ten *and* Bottom Ten

➤ *make sure you understand what the programme is doing*

➤ *are any countries consistently appearing in the top or bottom ten?*

Page 2 of teacher-prepared Balcarras study guide

Use **Map Ten**

➤ *can you identify any pattern in development?*

➤ *how would you describe the distribution of developing and developed countries?*

Compare the distribution of developing countries with patterns of malnutrition and average calorie intake

➤ *is there a relationship?*

➤ *why do you think this is so?*

Look at the relationships between the variables

➤ *are there any connections?*

➤ *is the calorie intake related to life expectancy? How?*

➤ *how many other connections can you see?*

***Look at* Scattergraph**

➤ *what is a Scattergraph?*

➤ *can you draw one?*

➤ *what do they show?*

➤ *when do you use one?*

Relationships

***Look at* Correlation**

➤ *what does it show?*

➤ *look at* **Development in the Third World page 14**

➤ *what is the Spearman Rank Correlation Test?*

➤ *arrange a tutorial to discuss this further*

Appendix D

An example of a pupil log book from Year 8
(See Chapter 2 page29)

WEEK COMMENCING: 10TH JUNE

	Planned Work	Resources	Actual Work
Lesson One	LOOK AT DEVELOPMENT DATA SEARCH. SEE WHAT A DEVELOPING COUNTRY IS.	DDS – INFO SHEET.	THOUGHT ABOUT THE ECONOMIC INDICATORS + MADE NOTES.
Homework	SORT OUT ROUGH NOTES AND WRITE THEM UP IN NEAT.	NOTEBOOK.	
Lesson Two	FIND OUT WHERE THE DEVELOPING COUNTRIES ARE – GLOBAL PATTERN.	DEVELOPMENT DATA SEARCH + ATLAS.	PLOTTED INFO ON A BLANK WORLD MAP.

Comments: Can you describe the global pattern?

Signed: McHughes,

WEEK COMMENCING: 17TH JUNE

	Planned Work	Resources	Actual Work
Lesson One	TUTORIAL WITH MR HUGHES TO FIND OUT ABOUT SPEARMAN RANK CORRELATION.	DEVELOPMENT IN THE THIRD WORLD BOOK (MICHAEL MORRISH p14)	TALKED ABOUT SPEARMAN RANK CORRELATION. WORKED THROUGH ON e.g WITH MR HUGHES.
Homework	TRY AND WORK OUT S.R.C.T BETWEEN CALORIE INTAKE AND LIFE EXPECTANCY.	NOTES TAKEN FROM DEVELOPMENT DATA SEARCH.	WORKED THROUGH IN ROUGH AND CALCULATED SPEARMAN RANK CORRELATION TEST.
Lesson Two	SHOW IT TO MR HUGHES HOW DO IT IN NEAT.	ROUGH NOTES.	

Comments: A very good week's work. It was obvious from our chat that you understood the idea of Spearman Rank Correlation.
Signed: I would like to see you try it with two other variables.
McHughes.

Appendix E

An example of a self-assessment sheet from Year 8

(See Chapter 2 page30)

ASSESSMENT

PUPILS COMMENT

THINGS I WAS PLEASED WITH Able to understand Spearman Rank Correlation I thought it would be too hard but after it was explained. I found it O.k. It was a good way to see if 2 variables were related.

THINGS I COULD HAVE IMPROVED

Disappointed that we didn't have much time because of disruption such as the French exchange.

STAFF COMMENT Yes, I was disappointed that various disruptions left you with little time to tack the Development unit. However you have still covered a large amount of material and in a significant depth. I was delighted with the way in which you tackled Spearman Rank correlation — it is an advanced technique and you handled it well. As ever, your approach and your presentation were **SKILLS COVERED** outstanding. Well done!

new skills ;   use of a database
                 Spearman Rank Correlation.
                 Scattergraphs (including best-fit line)

TARGET

I would like to see you employ the new techniques that you have been introduced to (scattergraphs and Spearman Rank) in a new situation. Remember, they can be used with any two related variables.

SIGNED PUPIL *(signature)*   **TEACHER** *(signature)* .DATE 5TH JULY

The Teaching and Learning Series

All books in the Teaching and Learning series £6.50. Discounts are available for bulk orders direct from the publishers. Order forms and further details from: Network Educational Press, PO Box 635, Stafford, ST17 OJR. Tel: 0785 225515.

This book, *Flexible Learning: Evidence Examined* is the sixth in the series and preceded by others which examine in more depth some of the issues raised.

Book 1, *Flexible learning: an Outline*, by **Philip Waterhouse** provides an outline of all the key questions in the debate on teaching and learning styles. He examines the rationale, contexts and methods of flexible learning:

- The National Curriculum
- Tutoring
- Assessment
- The flexible use of space, time, money and people

- TVEI
- The use of libraries and resource centres
- Records of Achievement
- Study skills.

Flexible Learning: an Outline is a handbook. Each chapter provides an agenda, a checklist of key issues and will be invaluable to all those interested in stimulating discussion or raising awareness on the subject of how teachers teach and how students learn.

ISBN 1 85539 003 5 £6.50

Book 2, *Classroom Management,* by **Philip Waterhouse**, provides a detailed insight into the management of a wide variety of teaching and learning strategies. It provides practical advice on:

- Planning and organisation of schemes of work
- Differentiation
- Assignments
- Management of resources
- The organisation and layout of classrooms
- Assessment and recording
- Managing whole-class, small-group and individual work.

The Book will be a valuable handbook for both classroom teachers and those managing teaching and learning in schools and colleges.

ISBN 1 85539 004 3 £6.50

Book 3, *Resources for Flexible Learning*, by **Robert Powell**, provides practical advice on the complex question of resources.

- Defining flexible resources
- Choosing and evaluating resources
- Adapting existing materials for differentiation
- Making full use of libraries/resource centres
- Preparing study guides
- Thinking about design and layout
- Using desktop publishing.

The book will suggest ways in which teachers and students can use a wide variety of resources both to satisfy the demands of the National Curriculum and to develop independent learning skills.

ISBN 1 85539 005 1 £6.50

Book 4, *Tutoring*, by **Philp Waterhouse** explores the possibilities of small-group tutoring. It presents clearly:

- The rationale and objectives of tutoring
- The context for tutoring
- Arrangements for tutoring
- Tutoring styles
- Tutoring techniques.

The book will serve as an invaluable handbook for all those in schools and colleges seeking to provide guidance and support to students both in the classroom and in more informal learning situations.

ISBN 1 85539 006 X £6.50

Book 5, *What Makes a Good School?* by **Tim Brighouse** identifies those features of school organisation and management which are essential elements of successful teaching and learning. It examines:

- Leadership in the successful school
- Environment in the successful school
- Staff development in the successful school
- Collective review in the successful school
- The organisation of learning in the successful school
- Successful teaching and learning.

ISBN 1 85539 007 8 £6.50

Study Guides from Network Educational Press

Study Guides support the development of high quality independent skills, project work, group work, core skills and cross-curricular themes.

Each Network Educational Press guide sets out in student friendly language:

- key learning objectives
- a resources section with ideas on where information can be found
- guidance on how students might plan and organise the work/enquiry
- key ideas, concepts or skills to be covered
- hints on ways in which students might present their findings
- a structure which links easily with records of achievement.

Each guide is photocopiable and allows students and teachers to record additional information - personal targets, assessment criteria, deadlines, length, etc.

Study guides are currently available in :

Key Stage 3	History
Key Stage 4	Geography, Business Studies, Humanities, English Literature, English Language
A Level	English Literature, History

Available Summer Term 1993

Key Stage 3	Modern Languages, Science
Key Stage 4	Science

Available during Autumn 1993

Key Stage 3/4	Technology
A Level	Geography, Physics, Chemistry, Biology, Economics, Business Studies, Sociology, Communications/Media, Psychology
GNVQ/NVQ	Business, Art and Design, Health and Beauty, Hotel and Catering, Travel, Tourism and Leisure, Hairdressing

Details of all these publications from:

Network Educational Press, PO Box 635, Stafford, ST17 OJR
Telephone: 0785 225515